AIR FRYER RECIPE BOOK

The Complete Air Fryer Cookbook | Delicious, Healthy and Quick Air Fryer Recipes For Everyone

Table of Contents

Introduction 7

What is an air fryer? 8

    Benefits... why use an air fryer? 8

    How to use it 9

Air Fryer Recipes 10

    Meat 11

        Spice-coated Steaks 12

        Lamb Steaks with Fresh Mint and Potatoes 13

        Pork and Apple Burger Patties 14

        Beef Quesadillas 15

        Pork Tenderloin with Apple and Cinnamon 16

        Meatloaf 17

        Spicy-sweet Beef and Veggie Stir Fry 18

        Mint and Fennel Lamb Meatballs 19

        Crispy Pork Chops 20

        Crunchy Beef Schnitzel 21

        Beef and Mushroom Pie 22

        Lamb, Pine Nut, Feta and Spice Pastry Pockets 23

    Poultry 24

        Chicken Parmigiana 25

        Crispy Breaded Chicken Tenders with Paprika Aioli 26

        Whole Roast Chicken with Bacon, Lemon and Rosemary 27

        Honey-mustard Drumsticks 28

        Turkey Burgers 29

        Stuffed Chicken Breast 30

        Green Curry Chicken Thighs 31

Coconut and Peanut Chicken Skewers 32
Homemade Chicken Nuggets 33
Sesame-crusted Wings 34
Chicken Bites with Cornflake Coating 35
Chili Chicken 36

Seafood **37**
Crispy Fish Finger 38
Spice-coated Prawns 39
Air-fryer Salmon with Lemon Seasoning 40
Tuna Grilled Cheese 41
Healthier Fish and Chips 42
Crab Cakes 43
Breaded Scallops 44
Fish Pie 45
Chili-lime Salmon and Sesame Broccoli 46
Panko-coated Seafood Platter 47
Smoked Fish Quiche 48

Vegan & Vegetarian **49**
Roasted Veggies with Balsamic Dressing (Vegan and Vegetarian) 50
Corn Cakes (Vegetarian) 51
Baked Potatoes with Cheese and Corn Stuffing (Vegetarian) 52
Crunchy Fried Tofu (Vegan and Vegetarian) 53
Veggie Tacos (Vegetarian) 54
Fried Halloumi and Veggies (Vegetarian) 55
Tempura Veggies (Vegan and Vegetarian) 56
Air-fried Falafels (Vegan and Vegetarian) 58
Fried Polenta Fries (Vegetarian - can be made Vegan) 60
Fried Veggie Sushi (Vegan and Vegetarian) 61
Teriyaki Cauliflower (Vegan and Vegetarian) 63

Breakfast **64**
- Banana Bread 65
- Hash Browns 66
- Bacon and Egg Muffins 67
- Breakfast Berry Oat Bars 68
- Spinach, Mushroom and Feta Omelet 69
- Banana, Walnut and Chocolate Muffins 70
- Caramel-filled French Toast 71
- Ham, Spinach and Mozzarella Fried Sourdough Sandwiches 72
- Sweet Potato, Spinach and Cheddar Frittata 73
- Apricot and Almond Scones 74
- Pancetta-wrapped Asparagus Tarts 75

Appetizers **76**
- Garlic and Herb Potato Chips 77
- Air-fried Croquettes 78
- Stuffed Mushrooms with Cheese and Red Rice 79
- Smoked Fish Balls 80
- Spring Rolls 81
- Meatballs 82
- Pita Pizzas 83
- Spicy Fries 84
- Cheese and Olive Bruschetta 85
- Fried Ravioli 86
- Goat Cheese, Prune and Bacon Bombs 87
- Salmon Canape Tarts 88

Desserts **89**
- Chocolate and Strawberry Cake 90
- Cheaters Cookie Bars with Added Chocolate 91
- Sticky Cinnamon Rolls 92

Citrus Cheesecake 94
Stone Fruit Pie 95
Baked Apples 96
S'mores 97
Brownies 98
Berry and White Chocolate Mini Cheesecakes 99
Cheats Apple and Caramel Crumble Cake 100
Chocolate and Banana Brioche Sandwiches 101

Conclusion 102

Introduction

Greetings, air fryer owners!

Whether you're a complete air fryer newbie or you simply want a few more ideas for tasty meals to make in your air fryer, you're sure to find this book handy.

Air fryers are absolutely genius appliances, especially for people who love yummy food but don't love all the oil and fat which usually accompanies it.

The recipes in this book are designed to be suitable for any air fryer of any brand, construction and design. If you need to adjust the quantities, temperature or time to suit your particular air fryer model, you absolutely can!

We have recipes for meat, poultry, seafood, vegan & vegetarian, breakfast, appetizers and desserts. Speaking of breakfast and desserts...you may notice that many of the recipes are completely decadent and full of naughty ingredients. I'll warn you now, this book isn't for those who are dieting. Or perhaps it is. Perhaps this is a great cheat-day cookbook! In saying that, you will find some healthy options too. It's all about balance, right?

Let's get into the air fryer ins and outs!

What is an air fryer?

An air fryer is a countertop cooking appliance which uses the circulation of very hot air to cook and fry foods. The aim is to get the same or similar result as a deep-fryer would but without the extra fat. Many air fryers also have baking, roasting, broiling, steaming and rotisserie functions too. Some people use their air fryer as an oven and microwave as they find it faster, easier and healthier.

The only setback is that you can't cook very soupy or liquid-dense foods in an air fryer as it can be dangerous. However, you can totally use marinades and batters, so fear not!

But what are the key benefits of an air fryer?

Benefits... why use an air fryer?

Less oil and fat
The number one reason people tend to gravitate toward air fryers is because they cut down the amount of fat and oil used during cooking. Instead of plunging your fries or spring rolls into a pot of boiling oil, you can pop them into the air fryer with a tablespoon (if that!) of oil. They'll be surrounded by hot air which makes the outside of the food crispy, while keeping the inside soft.

Not only do air fryers cut down the need to buy copious amounts of oil and fat, they cut down the number of calories you consume on a daily basis. You can enjoy the same foods but without the health-destroying side effects. Fries on a diet? Yup. Not that life is about dieting, but it is about being the healthiest we can be whilst still enjoying life's tastiest treats.

Neat, tidy and compact
Most air fryers are designed to be neat, compact and tidy as they sit on your countertop. This means that you can cook a wide range of foods without cluttering your kitchen bench. The cooking equipment (i.e. baskets and trays) can be stored inside the unit itself, eliminating the amount of clutter in your kitchen.

Versatile and easy
Most air fryers have many different functions which means you can basically put your oven and microwave into retirement. They are also super simple to use. This is encouraging for people who like to cook but don't want to fuss around with fiddly processes, ovens, microwaves and cooktops. Just prep the ingredients, put them in the air fryer, jiggle some dials, give the food a quick toss then enjoy your perfectly-cooked creations.

How to use it

Air fryers really are SO easy to use! But here's a quick how-to.

Find your recipe
Find a tasty recipe which is compatible with an air fryer. Most things which can be cooked in an oven or microwave can be cooked in an air fryer as long as they do not contain lots of liquid or fat. If unsure, use an air fryer cookbook like this one!

Choose your equipment
Figure out what the recipe requires from your air fryer. Does it need a basket, rack or rotisserie prongs? Do you need a cake tin, tart pans or muffin pan? If using equipment which isn't included in your air fryer, ensure that it fits and that it is safe for the air fryer.

Add your ingredients
Now it's time to follow the recipe and prepare your ingredients.

Add the ingredients to the basket, trays or racks. To prevent sticking, use baking paper or an oil spray.

Don't overfill or crowd the air fryer! Figure out if you need to do multiple batches in order to safely and thoroughly cook all of your food.

Select the time and temperature
Use the manual or digital temperature and time controls to adjust the temperature and time required for your recipe. Otherwise, you can use preset buttons which correspond with your recipe.

Check and shake the food
The recipe may state (many do) that you must give your food a shake, toss or turn during the cooking process. This prevents sticking and allows for even cooking with crispiness all around.

Switch the unit off, wait to cool and give it a clean
After the cooking process is over, unplug your air fryer and allow it to cool completely. Clean the parts according to the instructions for your specific model. Remember not to use harsh or abrasive tools or products on non-stick baskets and trays.

Air Fryer Recipes

Which type of air fryer are these recipes suitable for?
These recipes can be made in any air fryer! You may have a drawer-style air fryer (the type with the basket and handle), or an oven-style air fryer (with horizontal racks). Both are fine.

I have created these recipes with a simple air fryer in mind, the type that has a temperature dial and a timer dial only. However, if your air fryer has pre-set functions or specific food settings (i.e. roast, bake, broil etc.) you can use those functions too. You know your air fryer the best, so choose the functions and settings you feel are best for each dish, otherwise just use the manual settings to follow what the recipes suggest.

Rack or basket?
Some air fryers have a square cavity with layered racks. Others have a rounded basket with dividers or one simple cavity. Use whichever you have, the recipes are suitable for all models. All recipes give the option of "air fryer basket or rack" which reminds you that you can use whichever your air fryer comes with.

Timing
Air fryers can differ in terms of temperature. This means that it's wise to check your dishes early on in the cooking process to ensure they don't overcook. If you feel as though you won't need all of the time specified in the recipe, just cut the time down by a few minutes. Take the time recommendations as hints not hard-and-fast rules!

Oil spray
Most recipes require oil spray. You can either use the store bought oil spray in the can (i.e. PAM) or you can make your own by pouring olive oil into a spray bottle. Oil spray allows you to use only a tiny amount and distribute it evenly over the food or the basket and trays.

Meat

These recipes are designed to get the best out of your meat. Whether it's beef, pork or lamb you can expect a tender, tasty result with lots of flavor and a super-simple method.

Spice-coated Steaks

Thick, juicy steaks coated in a mixture of warming spice, salt and pepper. I like to slice the steaks diagonally before serving either as the main event of a salad or with a side of fresh veggies. This recipe should result in a medium-rare steak, depending on the thickness of your meat. Add a couple of minutes to the cook time if you like your steak well done.

Serves: 4
Time: approximately 12 minutes

Ingredients:
- 2 large, thick steaks
- 1 Tbsp. olive oil
- ½ tsp. ground cumin
- ½ tsp. ground chili
- ½ tsp. ground paprika
- Salt and pepper

Method:
1. Preheat your air fryer if it requires pre-heating.
2. Place the steaks onto a board and leave to reach room temperature if they've just come out of the fridge.
3. Rub the olive oil, cumin, chili, paprika, salt and pepper over the steaks and massage it in, ensuring an even coating.
4. Place the steaks into your air fryer rack, basket or pan and place into the air fryer cavity.
5. Adjust the temperature to 400 degrees Fahrenheit and adjust the time to 6 minutes.
6. At the 3-minute mark, slip the basket or rack out of the air fryer, turn the steaks and slip the basket/rack back into the unit.
7. When the timer rings out, remove the steaks from the air fryer and leave to rest on a board for a few minutes.
8. Enjoy with mash, mushrooms, salad…whatever takes your fancy!

Lamb Steaks with Fresh Mint and Potatoes

Lamb and mint make such a beautiful pair. And what better accompaniment for them than potatoes? Add some freshly-boiled peas and carrots and you've got a truly classic dinner. I like to use the thickest lamb steaks I can find!

Serves: 4
Time: approximately 20 minutes including prep

Ingredients:
- 4 lamb steaks
- 1 Tbsp. olive oil (for the lamb steaks)
- 2 garlic cloves, crushed
- Salt and pepper
- Handful of fresh mint leaves (about 10 large leaves), roughly chopped
- 4 medium-large potatoes, cut into even chunks or cubes
- 1 Tbsp. olive oil (for the potatoes)
- Salt and pepper

Method:
1. Rub the lamb steaks with olive oil, crushed garlic, salt and pepper.
2. Place the mint leaves into your air fryer, either onto the tray or in the basket.
3. Lay the lamb steaks on top of the mint leaves.
4. Rub the potato chunks with olive oil and sprinkle with salt and pepper.
5. If you are using a single basket, place the potatoes next to the lamb steaks, or place them on a rack or tray below the lamb steaks.
6. Set the temperature to 400 degrees Fahrenheit and set the time to 12 minutes.
7. At the 6-minute mark, open the air fryer and turnover the lamb steaks and potatoes.
8. When the timer rings, check the steak and potatoes. If they're cooked to your liking, you're done! If they're not quite done yet, pop them back in for a further 2 minutes.
9. Enjoy with a fresh side salad.

Note: I discard the mint leaves once the cooking is done, I find that they infuse the lamb with sufficient mint flavour as the lamb cooks.

Pork and Apple Burger Patties

These patties make for a refreshing change to the usual burger. Apple adds delicious sweetness to the savory ground pork, and a touch of spice adds a gentle exotic flavor.

Serves: makes about 6 patties
Time: approximately 20 minutes

Ingredients:
- 17 oz. ground pork
- 1 apple, peeled and grated
- 1 cup breadcrumbs
- 2 eggs, lightly beaten
- ½ tsp. ground cumin
- ½ tsp. ground cinnamon
- Salt and pepper

Method:
1. Place the pork, apple, breadcrumbs, eggs, cumin, cinnamon, salt and pepper into a large bowl.
2. Use your hands (clean!) to thoroughly combine the mixture.
3. Shape the mixture into even-sized burger patties.
4. Spray your rack or basket with oil spray to prevent sticking.
5. Place the patties into your air fryer basket or onto the rack and close the lid/lock basket into place.
6. Set the temperature to 360 degrees Fahrenheit and set the time to 12 minutes.
7. At the 6-minute mark, open the air fryer and turn each patty.
8. Once the air fryer beeps, remove the patties and check if they're cooked to your liking, if not? Pop them back in for a couple of minutes.

Tip: use these patties to assemble a tasty burger with brioche buns, slaw and spicy mayo!

Beef Quesadillas

These quesadillas are cheesy, beefy and full of fresh cilantro and red chili. I like to serve them with sour cream and guacamole (I mean, of course). You can swap the beef for chicken if you like, just be extra careful that it's cooked all the way through.

Serves: 2 as a main, 4 as a starter
Time: approximately 25 minutes

Ingredients:
- 8 small soft round taco shells
- 1 beef steak, thinly sliced
- 1 cup grated cheese, use any you like but I generally use mozzarella
- 1/3 cup fresh cilantro, roughly chopped
- 1 red chili, finely chopped
- 1 cup corn kernels, canned or fresh
- Salt and pepper
- Oil spray

Method:
1. Lay the soft taco shells onto a board and sprinkle each one with sliced steak (the steak is thinly sliced so no need to pre-cook).
2. Sprinkle over the cheese, cilantro, chili, corn, salt and pepper.
3. Carefully fold each one in half (so it's a half-circle shape) and secure with toothpicks if you are worried about spillage in the air fryer.
4. Spray your basket or rack with oil spray to prevent sticking.
5. Place the filled quesadillas into the basket or onto the rack. If you can, double-layer the racks so the quesadillas have more room and don't overlap.
6. Close the door or click the basket into place.
7. Set the temperature to 360 degrees Fahrenheit and set the time to 15 minutes.
8. At the 7-minute mark, turn the quesadillas over.
9. Once the timer beeps, check the quesadillas to see if they're crispy enough for your liking and pop them back in for a further couple of minutes if need be.
10. Serve with all of your favorite Mexican sides and sauces!

Pork Tenderloin with Apple and Cinnamon

Yes, we have another pork recipe with apple and cinnamon. The combination is too good to miss. However, this recipe also has a hit of saltiness with the addition of soy sauce. I like to serve these pork tenderloins with fresh, crunchy slaw and either a soft bun or mashed potatoes (or opt for brown rice/sweet potatoes, but I'm all about embracing the white carbs every now and then!).

Serves: 4
Time: approximately 1 hour including marinating time

Ingredients:
- 4 pork tenderloins
- 1 apple, sliced into wedges
- 1 cinnamon quill
- 1 Tbsp. olive oil
- 1 Tbsp. soy sauce
- Salt and pepper

Method:
1. Place the pork, apple wedges, cinnamon quill, olive oil, soy sauce, salt and pepper into a bowl and stir until the pork and apple is coated in oil, sauce and seasoning.
2. Leave to marinate at room temperature for 30 minutes.
3. Place the pork and apples into the basket of your air fryer, or on a tray. You can include a bit of the oil and sauce but not too much. Just enough so that the meat is coated but not dripping.
4. Secure the basket back into the unit.
5. Set the temperature to 360 degrees Fahrenheit and the time to 15 minutes.
6. At the 7 or 8-minute mark, turn the tenderloins.
7. When the timer beeps, check the meat to ensure it is fully cooked, and cook for a further couple of minutes if not.
8. Serve hot!

Tip: you can use the cooked apples to make a delicious sauce or gravy by simmering them with a dash of soy sauce and enough water to make a sauce.

Meatloaf

Meatloaf always seems like such an old fashioned, uninspiring dish to me... until I make it and realise it's actually delicious and comforting. For total decadence, it's great served with fries (another use for your air fryer!) and a simple salad.

Serves: makes 1 meatloaf
Time: approximately 35 minutes

Ingredients:
- 1 lb. ground beef
- 2 eggs, lightly beaten
- ½ cup breadcrumbs
- 2 garlic cloves, crushed
- 1 brown onion, finely chopped
- 2 Tbsp. tomato paste
- 1 tsp. mixed dried herbs
- Salt and pepper

Method:
1. Prepare a loaf pan by lining with baking paper. Make sure it fits in your air fryer.
2. In a large bowl combine the beef, eggs, breadcrumbs, garlic, onions, tomato paste, dried herbs, salt and pepper.
3. Press the mixture into the prepared pan and place into the air fryer.
4. Set the temperature to 360 degrees Fahrenheit and set the time to 30 minutes.
5. When the timer beeps, check to see if the meatloaf is cooked but still moist inside, pop it back in for a few minutes if you feel as though it's not cooked enough.
6. Leave to rest for about 10 minutes before turning out and slicing.

Spicy-sweet Beef and Veggie Stir Fry

Good old beef stir-fry. It always comes to the rescue when I have no idea what to make for dinner. The air fryer is a great way to quickly cook your beef to perfection. Of course, this recipe is less saucy than other stir-fry recipes, but i actually prefer my stir-fries to be a little dryer but with plenty of spice and flavor.

Serves: 4
Time: approximately 20 minutes

Ingredients:
- 2 large beef steaks, sliced into thin strips
- 2 garlic cloves, finely chopped
- 2 tsp. honey
- 1 tsp. oyster sauce
- 1 tsp. chili powder
- ½ tsp. sesame oil
- Juice of 1 lime
- Salt and pepper
- 1 broccoli, cut into florets
- 2 carrots, cut into chunks
- 1 cup green beans

Method:
1. Place the beef, garlic, honey, oyster sauce, chili powder, sesame oil, lime juice, salt and pepper into a bowl and stir to combine.
2. Place the beef (with the garlic and some of the juices) into the basket of your air fryer and place the veggies on top. If you have an oven-style air fryer with trays, place the beef and veggies onto a tray.
3. Lock the basket into place or close the oven door.
4. Set the temperature to 360 degrees Fahrenheit and set the time to 10 minutes.
5. At the 5-minute mark, turn the meat and veggies.
6. When the timer beeps, check to see if the meat and veggies are cooked to your liking.
7. Enjoy with freshly-cooked rice and a drizzle of soy sauce.

Mint and Fennel Lamb Meatballs

Ground lamb makes the best meatballs ever. Dried mint and fennel seeds add depth of flavour, and the air fryer cooks them to perfection without all the fat and oil of a frying pan. I like to serve these with warmed pita breads, plain yogurt and sliced cucumber.

Serves: 3 (makes about 12-14 meatballs give or take depending on the size)
Time: approximately 15 minutes

Ingredients:
- 1 lb. ground lamb
- 1 brown onion, finely chopped
- 2 garlic cloves, finely chopped
- ½ cup shredded or grated mozzarella cheese
- 1 egg, lightly beaten
- 1 Tbsp. balsamic vinegar
- ½ tsp. dried mint
- ½ tsp. fennel seed
- Salt and pepper
- Oil spray

Method:
1. Place the lamb, onion, garlic, cheese, egg, balsamic vinegar, mint, fennel, salt and pepper into a large bowl and mix with your hands until thoroughly combined.
2. Roll the mixture into balls (approximately the size of golf balls) and set aside.
3. Spray your air fryer basket or tray with oil spray to prevent sticking.
4. Place the meatballs onto the basket, tray or rack.
5. Secure the basket into the unit or close the door.
6. Set the temperature to 350 degrees Fahrenheit and set the time to 10 minutes.
7. Check the meatballs to see if they are done to your liking. I like mine to be a little pink in the centre, but you can adjust the time to suit your preference!
8. Serve however you like, but I can't get over pita and yogurt dressing.

Crispy Pork Chops

This is a very simple recipe which results in crispy, tasty pork chops. I add a hint of paprika to mine, but that's optional. Great for an easy weeknight dinner served with mashed potatoes and slaw, or a simple salad and fresh rolls.

Serves: 4 (1 pork chop each, you can halve or double the recipe but you will need to do more than one batch if you do more than 4 pork chops)

Time: approximately 25 minutes

Ingredients:
- 4 pork chops
- 2 Tbsp. flour
- ½ tsp. paprika (optional, but I like the smokiness)
- 2 Tbsp. buttermilk
- Salt and pepper
- 1/3 cup breadcrumbs (may need more or less depending on size of your pork chops, just enough to coat them thoroughly)
- Oil spray

Method:
1. Lightly coat the pork chops with flour (if using paprika, combine it with the flour first).
2. Drizzle the buttermilk over the floured pork chops and gently rub it in to coat each piece.
3. Spread the breadcrumbs onto a plate and coat each pork chop thoroughly with breadcrumbs.
4. Spray the coated pork chops with oil spray.
5. Place the pork chops into the basket or onto the rack/tray in your air fryer.
6. Secure the air fryer closed.
7. Set the temperature to 350 degrees Fahrenheit and set the time to 15 minutes.
8. At the 7-minute mark, turn the chops over.
9. Once the timer beeps, check the chops to see if they're cooked to your liking, and pop them back in for an extra couple of minutes if need be.
10. Serve with slaw and mashed potatoes!

Crunchy Beef Schnitzel

Beef schnitzel is one of the best comfort foods of all time, especially when served with a hearty serving of fries! All you need is schnitzel beef cutlets (or just thin minute steaks), flour, egg, breadcrumbs and seasoning.

Serves: 4
Time: approximately 20 minutes

Ingredients:
- 4 beef schnitzel cutlets (not crumbed)
- ½ cup flour (may not need it all)
- 2 eggs, lightly beaten
- Salt and pepper
- 1 cup breadcrumbs (may not need the whole cup but you can always save the leftover crumbs)
- Zest of one lemon (optional)
- Oil spray

Method:
1. Coat the beef cutlets in flour and shake off any excess.
2. Dip the coated cutlets into the beaten egg and let any excess drip away.
3. Sprinkle with salt and pepper (it will stick to the egg so now is a good time to season).
4. If using lemon zest, add it to the breadcrumbs.
5. Dip the cutlets into the breadcrumbs and ensure they are thoroughly coated.
6. Spray the breaded schnitzels generously with oil spray.
7. Place the schnitzels into the basket or onto the tray of your air fryer.
8. Secure the basket closed or close the air fryer door.
9. Set the temperature to 390 degrees Fahrenheit and set the time to 8 minutes.
10. Turn the schnitzels over at the 4-minute mark.
11. Once the timer beeps, check the schnitzels to see if they are cooked to your liking, pop them back in for another minute or two if need be.

Beef and Mushroom Pie

These pies are rich and meaty, great for a Winter's evening. They only have pastry on the top, but you can adjust the recipe and have them fully cased in pastry if you wish. I use store bought pastry... it's just so easy.

Serves: makes 1 pie, about 4 servings (but it depends on the size of your pie pan and air fryer cavity)
Time: approximately 50 minutes

Ingredients:
- 1 sheet store bought (or homemade if you wish) shortcrust pastry
- 1 Tbsp. olive oil
- 1 lb. steak, cubed
- 1 onion, roughly chopped
- 2 Tbsp. flour
- 2 cups chopped mushrooms
- 1/3 cup red wine
- 1 beef stock cube
- ½ cup water
- Salt and pepper

Method:
1. Prepare a pie dish by spraying with oil spray. Ensure the pie dish fits in your air fryer.
2. Drizzle the olive oil into a large pot or pan and place over a medium-high heat.
3. Add the beef and stir until browned.
4. Add the onions and stir as they become translucent.
5. Stir the flour into the pot until the beef cubes are coated.
6. Stir the mushrooms into the pot and allow them to cook for a couple of minutes.
7. Add the red wine, stock cube, water, salt and pepper to the pot and stir until thoroughly combined.
8. Allow the mixture to come to a simmer and stir occasionally, adding a dash of water if it becomes too dry. Simmer for about 20 minutes.
9. Pour the beef mixture into your pie dish and place the sheet of pastry over the top, trim the edges, press the edges into the sides of the pan and cut a few slits into the top to allow steam to escape.
10. Place the pie dish into your air fryer.
11. Set the temperature to 350 degrees Fahrenheit and set the time to 10 minutes.
12. Once the timer beeps, check the pie. The pastry should be flaky and golden.
13. Serve with fresh greens and tomato ketchup!

Lamb, Pine Nut, Feta and Spice Pastry Pockets

These little parcels are filled with ground lamb, pine nuts, spices and raisins. Yes, you can leave the raisins out if you don't like them! These parcels are a lovely starter or light meal, and can be dipped into sauces such as mint-yogurt.

Serves: makes 8 small parcels
Time: approximately 30 minutes

Ingredients:
- 8 store bought filo pastry sheets,
- 1 lb. ground lamb
- ½ onion, finely chopped
- 3 Tbsp. pine nuts
- 3 Tbsp. raisins
- 4 oz. feta cheese, crumbled or roughly chopped
- ½ tsp. ground cinnamon
- ½ tsp. ground cumin
- Salt and pepper
- 1 egg, lightly beaten
- Oil spray

Method:
1. Combine the lamb, onion, pine nuts, raisins, feta, cinnamon, cumin, salt and pepper in a bowl. If you can, try to roughly portion the mixture into 8 portions but no need to be too precise.
2. Lay the filo sheets out onto a clean board (you'll have to do 1 or 2 at a time depending on how much space you've got).
3. Place a portion of lamb mixture into the centre of each pastry sheet. Fold the pastry over the lamb mixture, then wrap it like a present until it becomes a compact package. There's no set method, just wrap it on up!
4. Brush the packages with the beaten egg then spray with oil spray.
5. Place the packages into the basket or onto the tray in your air fryer and secure the air fryer closed.
6. Set the temperature to 320 degrees Fahrenheit and set the time to 8 minutes.
7. At the 4-minute mark, turn the packages.
8. Once the timer beeps, check the packages to ensure they are golden and crispy!
9. Serve with yogurt and mint dressing, fresh salad and warm flat breads.

Poultry

Air fryers and chicken go together so well. In fact, many people buy an air fryer especially so they can make healthier fried chicken! There are a few crispy, crunchy recipes in this collection as well as a few stickier, sweeter options.

Chicken Parmigiana

This recipe cheats a little bit as it uses store bought marinara sauce. You can make your own, of course, but you only need a small amount so make sure you've got a use for the rest of it. Parmesan and mozzarella cheese melt on top of tender chicken and tangy marinara sauce... delicious.

Serves: 2
Time: approximately 20 minutes

Ingredients:

- 2 chicken breasts (skinless), beaten with a mallet or rolling pin: ensure the breasts are an even thickness, about ½ an inch
- 1 egg, lightly beaten
- ½ cup breadcrumbs mixed with salt and pepper
- 2 Tbsp. store bought or homemade marinara sauce
- 2 Tbsp. parmesan cheese, grated
- 2 slices mozzarella cheese

Method:

1. Dip the chicken breasts into the beaten egg.
2. Dip the egg-coated chicken into the breadcrumbs until thoroughly coated.
3. Place the breaded chicken breasts into your air fryer (either in the basket or on the rack).
4. Set the temperature to 390 degrees Fahrenheit and set the time to 5 minutes.
5. When the timer beeps, turn the chicken breasts over and top them both with marinara sauce, parmesan and mozzarella cheese.
6. Set the time to 5 minutes (reset the temperature to 390 if your air fryer switches off).
7. When the timer beeps, check to ensure the chicken is cooked all the way through.
8. Serve with salad, rolls, potatoes... or anything your heart desires.

Crispy Breaded Chicken Tenders with Paprika Aioli

These breaded chicken tenders are so simple to prepare and cook. With a touch of garlic powder and chili for depth, and a tasty aioli dipping sauce to add that extra flair.

Serves: makes approximately 16 tenders (about 4 per person)
Time: approximately 20 minutes (which includes cooking in 3 batches)

Ingredients:
- 3 large chicken breasts (skinless), cut into tenders (even-sized strips)
- Oil spray
- ¾ cup breadcrumbs
- Salt and pepper
- ½ tsp. garlic powder
- ½ tsp. ground chili

Aioli:
- 1/3 cup plain aioli or mayonnaise
- ½ tsp. sweet or smoked paprika

Method:
1. Spray the chicken tenders with olive oil.
2. Combine the breadcrumbs, salt, pepper, garlic powder and chili and spread onto a plate.
3. Roll the oiled chicken tenders in the breadcrumb mixture until thoroughly coated.
4. Spray the breaded tenders with a touch of oil.
5. Place a single layer of tenders into your air fryer, either in the basket or on the rack.
6. Set the temperature to 390 degrees Fahrenheit and set the time to 5 minutes.
7. At the 2-minute mark, turn the chicken tenders.
8. Once the timer beeps, check the tenders to ensure they are cooked all the way through, and crispy on the outside. They may need a little more cooking depending on the thickness.
9. Cook the tenders in batches until they're all cooked.
10. To make the paprika aioli: combine the aioli or mayo with the paprika.
11. Serve the tenders hot or warm, with a side dish of paprika aioli.

Whole Roast Chicken with Bacon, Lemon and Rosemary

A whole roast chicken always looks so tasty and impressive when really, it's one of the simplest things in the world to cook. This one has bacon, lemon and rosemary nestled in the cavity. Once you've devoured the meat, use the carcass to make a tasty broth by boiling in water with onions, carrots and herbs until rich. Use your air fryer rotisserie function if it has one.

Serves: makes 1 whole chicken
Time: approximately 1 hour

Ingredients:

- 1 whole chicken, make sure it fits into your air fryer without overcrowding it
- 1 lemon
- 5 rashers of streaky bacon, roughly chopped
- 1 onion, roughly chopped
- 1 sprig fresh rosemary
- Oil spray
- Salt and pepper

Method:

1. In a small bowl combine the bacon, onion and rosemary, season with salt and pepper.
2. Pat the chicken with a dry paper towel until the skin is nice and dry.
3. Reach the bacon mixture into the cavity of the chicken and press it in tight.
4. Stuff the lemon (whole) into the cavity.
5. Rub the top and sides of the chicken generously with salt and pepper.
6. Spray the basket or tray of your air fryer generously with oil spray.
7. Place the chicken into the basket or onto the tray.
8. Set the temperature to 390 degrees Fahrenheit and set the time to 30 minutes.
9. When the timer rings, turn the chicken over and pop it back into the air fryer for a further 15-20 minutes but you can check it throughout the cooking time to ensure it doesn't dry or overcook.
10. Serve hot or cold, in a sandwich or with roasted veggies for a traditional Sunday dinner!

Honey-mustard Drumsticks

Sticky, sweet, savory and very easy to make. These drumsticks are perfect for a picnic lunch, Summertime dinner with salad, or cold out of the fridge for a cheeky snack.

Serves: 4 (2 drumsticks each)
Time: approximately 30 minutes

Ingredients:
- 8 drumsticks
- 3 Tbsp. honey
- 2 Tbsp. dijon mustard
- ½ tsp. garlic powder
- Salt and pepper

Method:
1. Combine the honey, mustard, garlic powder, salt and pepper in a large bowl.
2. Add the drumsticks to the bowl and stir until every drumstick is coated in sauce.
3. Lay the coated drumsticks into your air fryer, ensuring that they are not too crowded, depending on the size of your air fryer, you may need to do more than one batch.
4. Set the temperature to 380 degrees Fahrenheit and set the timer to 20 minutes.
5. At the 10-minute mark, turn the drumsticks over.
6. Once the timer beeps, check to ensure the chicken is cooked all the way through.
7. Enjoy!

Turkey Burgers

These turkey burger patties are a simple and tasty alternative to the more common beef or chicken burgers. They have a hit of spice and a sprinkle of breadcrumbs to bulk them out. I like to use brioche buns, cheese, lettuce, tomato and mayo to create a classic, yummy burger. But you can make anything you like with these delicious patties!

Serves: makes 8 patties (halve the mixture if you only need 4 patties)
Time: approximately 20 minutes

Ingredients:
- 1 lb. ground turkey
- ½ onion, finely chopped
- 2 garlic cloves, finely chopped
- 1 egg, lightly beaten
- 1/3 cup breadcrumbs
- ½ tsp. ground cumin
- ½ tsp. ground chili
- ½ tsp. ground coriander (or crushed cilantro seeds)
- Salt and pepper

Method:
1. Combine the turkey, onion, garlic, egg, breadcrumbs, cumin, chili, coriander, salt and pepper in a large bowl. I find my hands are the best tools for mixing ground meats.
2. Shape the mixture into 8 even-sized patties.
3. Spray your air fryer basket or tray with oil spray.
4. Place the patties into the basket or onto the tray, careful not to layer them or overcrowd the cavity.
5. Set the temperature to 340 degrees Fahrenheit and set the time to 10 minutes.
6. Once the timer beeps, check the patties to ensure they're cooked to your liking and pop them back in if you feel they need a little more cooking time.
7. Assemble your burgers with your favorite ingredients!

Stuffed Chicken Breast

Juicy chicken breasts stuffed with cheese, basil and sundried tomatoes. These are quite filling so I find that one large chicken breast is enough for two people, especially if you're serving it with warm rolls, veggies and whichever tasty side dishes you fancy!

Serves: 4 (half a large chicken breast per serving)
Time: approximately 25-30 minutes

Ingredients:

- 2 large chicken breasts (skinless)
- 2 thick slices of cheese (I use mozzarella)
- 4 fresh basil leaves
- 4 large sun dried tomatoes, roughly chopped
- Salt and pepper
- Oil spray

Method:

1. Cut a slit into the side of each chicken breast, but don't cut all the way through. You're aiming for a "pocket" into which you can stuff your stuffing ingredients.
2. Press a slice of cheese into the cavity of each chicken breast and follow with 2 basil leaves and half of the sun dried tomatoes.
3. Use toothpicks to keep the chicken breasts closed if you feel the filling is going to spill out.
4. Sprinkle the breasts with salt and pepper and spray with oil spray.
5. Give the air fryer basket or tray a gentle spray with the oil spray too.
6. Place the chicken breasts into the basket or onto the tray.
7. Set the temperature to 370 degrees Fahrenheit and set the time to 10 minutes.
8. Once the timer beeps at the 10-minute mark, turn the breasts over.
9. Cook for a further 5 minutes then check to see if they're cooked all the way through, or if they need a few more minutes. Every air fryer brand is different and the thickness of the chicken also makes a difference to the cook time, so use your discretion here!
10. Slice each chicken breast in half and serve with fresh veggies, a fresh roll and a side of fries if you're feeling a bit decadent!

Green Curry Chicken Thighs

Sometimes I like to use curry paste to flavor my chicken, without all the coconut cream and simmering involved in a proper curry. I still get the flavor but in an easier fashion. This recipe does use a little bit of coconut cream but not much at all, just enough to provide flavor and moisture.

Serves: 4 - 6
Time: approximately 20 minutes

Ingredients:
- 8 chicken thighs, boneless, skinless
- 2 Tbsp. green curry paste (a good store bought paste is absolutely fine, ideal in fact!)
- 3 Tbsp. coconut cream
- Salt and pepper
- ½ fresh red chili, finely chopped
- Handful fresh cilantro, roughly chopped

Method:
1. Place the chicken thighs, curry paste, coconut cream, salt, pepper and chili into a large bowl and stir until the chicken thighs are evenly coated.
2. Place the coated chicken thighs into your air fryer basket or rack, ideally in a single layer.
3. Set the time to 350 degrees Fahrenheit and set the time to 8 minutes.
4. Once the timer beeps, check the chicken to ensure it is cooked all the way through, if not, pop it back for a further couple of minutes.
5. Serve with the fresh cilantro and some fluffy white rice.

Coconut and Peanut Chicken Skewers

Chicken skewers are fun, easy and delicious for dinner, snacks or as a starter at a party. These ones combine the creaminess of coconut cream and the salty nuttiness of peanut butter.

Serves: makes 8 skewers (about 2 per serving as a light dinner or lunch)
Time: approximately 20 minutes

Ingredients:
- 4 large chicken breasts (skinless), cut into even-sized chunks or cubes
- 4 Tbsp. coconut cream
- 4 Tbsp. crunchy or smooth peanut butter
- 1 Tbsp. soy sauce
- 1 Tbsp. fresh lime juice or lemon juice
- ½ tsp. ground chili
- Salt and pepper
- 8 skewers (make sure they fit in your air fryer)

Method:
1. In a large bowl combine the coconut cream, peanut butter, soy sauce, lime or lemon juice, chili, salt and pepper.
2. Take out half of the mixture from the bowl and set aside in a small cup or bowl.
3. Add the chopped chicken to the large bowl (with the original batch of sauce) and stir until the chicken is thoroughly coated in sauce.
4. Load your skewers with sauce-coated chicken until all 8 are filled.
5. Lay the skewers into the basket or onto the rack of your air fryer.
6. Set the temperature to 340 degrees Fahrenheit and the time to 15 minutes.
7. At the 7-minute mark, turn the skewers over.
8. Once the timer beeps, check the chicken to ensure it is cooked all the way through.
9. Brush the remaining sauce (which you reserved at the start) over the cooked chicken.
10. Serve with steamed broccoli and rice, or as a simple starter or party snack!

Homemade Chicken Nuggets

Chicken nuggets never go out of style, no matter your age or stage in life. There's something about those little golden morsels that make every meat-eater's mouth water. These ones are homemade, healthy and crisp. I serve mine with ketchup and garlic aioli.

Serves: 4 as a snack or starter
Time: approximately 15 minutes

Ingredients:
- 2 large chicken breasts (skinless), cut into nuggets
- 4 Tbsp. buttermilk
- ½ cup breadcrumbs
- ½ tsp. garlic powder
- ½ tsp. paprika
- Salt and pepper
- Oil spray

Method:
1. Place the chicken into a bowl and add the buttermilk, stir to combine.
2. Combine the breadcrumbs, garlic powder, paprika, salt and pepper and spread out onto a plate.
3. Roll the chicken pieces in the breadcrumbs until coated.
4. Spray your air fryer basket or tray with oil spray.
5. Lay the chicken nuggets into the basket or tray in a single layer (use a divider tray if you can, or do multiple batches).
6. Set the temperature to 390 degrees Fahrenheit and set the time to 8 minutes.
7. At the 4-minute mark, quickly turn the chicken nuggets over.
8. Once the timer beeps, check to ensure the chicken is cooked all the way through.
9. Serve with your favorite dipping sauces!

Sesame-crusted Wings

These wings are sticky, sweet and full of sesame flavor. The sesame seeds create a tasty, crunchy coating with a nutty taste. Great as a party snack, starter or basis of a light meal.

Serves: about 4
Time: approximately 20 minutes (or more if you need to do multiple batches)

Ingredients:
- 1 lb. chicken wings
- 1 tsp. sesame oil
- 2 tsp. honey
- Salt and pepper
- 2 Tbsp. sesame seeds (may need more)

Method:
1. Place the chicken wings, sesame oil, honey, salt and pepper into a large bowl and stir until every chicken wing has been coated.
2. Spread the sesame seeds onto a plate and roll each chicken wing in the seeds until coated.
3. Lay the chicken wings in a single layer into your air fryer basket or rack (you may need to do multiple batches depending on your air fryer capacity).
4. Set the temperature to 380 degrees Fahrenheit and set the time to 10 minutes.
5. Once the timer beeps, check to ensure the chicken is cooked all the way through.
6. Serve with soy sauce for dipping!

Chicken Bites with Cornflake Coating

If you've got a box of cornflakes sitting in your pantry, use them to make these tasty, crispy chicken bites! The cornflakes create a great texture to coat the tender, juicy chicken. Kids love these as much as adults do!

Serves: makes about 12 bites (3 or 4 per serving)
Time: approximately 20 minutes

Ingredients:

- 3 large chicken breasts, skinless, cut into 4 pieces each
- 1 egg, lightly beaten
- ¼ cup buttermilk
- 1 cup cornflakes, gently crushed
- Salt and pepper
- Oil spray

Method:

1. Whisk together the egg and buttermilk in a large bowl.
2. Add the chicken pieces to the bowl and stir to thoroughly coat in egg and buttermilk.
3. Spread the cornflakes out onto a plate and mix the salt and pepper into them.
4. Roll the chicken pieces in the cornflakes until coated.
5. Spray your air fryer basket or tray with oil spray.
6. Lay the coated chicken pieces in one layer onto your tray or into the basket.
7. Set the temperature to 380 degrees Fahrenheit and set the time to 10 minutes.
8. At the 5-minute mark, turn the chicken pieces over.
9. Once the timer beeps, check to ensure the chicken is cooked all the way through.
10. Serve with your favorite dipping sauces!

Chili Chicken

If you don't like chili... I'd skip this recipe! Fresh chili AND sweet chili sauce coat tender chicken thighs. I usually serve this dish with coconut rice and steamed broccoli (my go-to side dishes for chicken!).

Serves: 4
Time: approximately 25 minutes

Ingredients:
- 8 chicken thighs, boneless
- 3 garlic cloves, crushed
- 1 fresh red chili, finely chopped
- 3 Tbsp. sweet chili sauce
- Salt and pepper

Method:
1. Place the chicken thighs, garlic, red chili, sweet chili sauce, salt and pepper into a large bowl and stir until the chicken is thoroughly coated.
2. Place the chicken in a single layer into your air fryer basket or onto the tray.
3. Set the temperature to 380 degrees Fahrenheit and set the time to 10 minutes.
4. Once the timer beeps, check the to ensure the chicken is cooked all the way through, pop it back in for a couple of minutes if it needs a little more time.
5. Enjoy!

Seafood

These recipes really embrace the tenderness, sweetness and delicate flavor of seafood. Some recipes are really simple, with only a few ingredients to allow the beauty of the seafood to shine bright. Be careful to check on your seafood dishes early on in the cooking process just in case your air fryer is a little hotter or stronger which could lead to overcooked seafood. And of course, fresh seafood is best, but use frozen in a pinch!

Crispy Fish Finger

I like my crispy fish fingers to be very simple as I want the flavor of the fish to be the main event. You can add herbs and spices to the crumb mix if you like, but i keep mine nice and plain.

Serves: makes about 12 fish fingers
Time: approximately 15 minutes (more or less depending on the thickness of your fish)

Ingredients:
- 2 large fresh white fish filets, cut into 6 fingers each
- 1 egg, lightly beaten
- 1/3 cup buttermilk
- ¾ cup panko breadcrumbs
- Salt and pepper
- Oil spray

Method:
1. Combine the egg and buttermilk in a small bowl.
2. Dip the fish fingers into the egg mixture and allow the excess to drip away.
3. Combine the panko crumbs, salt and pepper and spread onto a plate.
4. Roll the egg-coated fish fingers in the crumbs until thoroughly coated.
5. Spray each finger with oil spray.
6. Place the fingers into the air fryer basket or rack.
7. Set the temperature to 350 degrees Fahrenheit and set the time to 8 minutes.
8. At the 4-minute mark, turn each fish finger.
9. Serve with garlic aioli and a squeeze of lemon.

Spice-coated Prawns

These prawns take barely any time to prepare, and less than 10 minutes to cook. They're ideal as a snack or for whenever you're craving seafood and spice.

Serves: makes 12 large prawns (about 3 per person as a light meal or snack)
Time: approximately 10 minutes

Ingredients:
- 12 large fresh prawns, cleaned
- Salt and pepper
- ½ tsp. chili powder
- ½ tsp. chili flakes
- ½ tsp. ground cumin
- ½ tsp. garlic powder
- Oil spray

Method:
1. Place the prawns into a bowl and toss with salt and pepper.
2. Add the chili powder, chili flakes, cumin and garlic powder and toss to combine, ensuring the prawns are coated.
3. Spray your air fryer basket or rack with oil spray and lay the prawns in a single layer onto the basket or rack.
4. Set the temperature to 360 degrees Fahrenheit and set the time to 6 minutes.
5. Once the timer beeps, check to ensure the prawns are cooked to your liking, and pop them back in if they need a couple more minutes.
6. Serve with sweet chili sauce or wrap them in fresh lettuce leaves!

Air-fryer Salmon with Lemon Seasoning

Salmon is such a rich and satisfying fish, it doesn't need much in the way of added flavor. This recipe uses only a few ingredients: salt, pepper and lemon zest. This recipe also works for other types of fish, but if they are thin filets, cut the cooking time down by a few minutes.

Serves: 4
Time: approximately 20 minutes

Ingredients:
- 4 salmon filets
- Oil spray
- Salt and pepper
- Zest of one lemon

Method:
1. Spray your salmon filets with oil spray.
2. Sprinkle the salt, pepper and lemon zest over the salmon and rub into the flesh.
3. To avoid sticking you can use baking paper to line your basket or tray.
4. Place the salmon filets into the basket or tray of your air fryer (skin-side down).
5. Set the temperature to 380 degrees Fahrenheit and set the time to 8 minutes.
6. When the timer beeps, check the salmon to ensure it is cooked to your liking.
7. Serve with fresh, seasonal veggies and a drizzle of olive oil!

Tuna Grilled Cheese

Time for cheesy, creamy comfort food. These tuna grilled cheese sandwiches (or tuna melts, if you prefer) have a dash of mayo for extra gooiness, and onion for savory sweetness. Use any cheese you like.

Serves: 2
Time: approximately 10 minutes

Ingredients:
- 4 slices of thick white bread
- 2 small tins of tuna, drained
- ½ small brown onion, finely chopped
- 2 Tbsp. creamy, full-fat mayonnaise
- Salt and pepper
- 1 cup grated cheese
- Oil spray

Method:
1. Lay your bread out onto a board.
2. Combine the tuna, onion, mayonnaise, salt and pepper in a small bowl.
3. Spread the tuna mixture over two of your bread slices.
4. Top the tuna mixture with the cheese and place the other piece of bread on top to create a sandwich.
5. Spray each side of the sandwich with oil spray (you'll have to turn them over carefully).
6. Place the sandwiches into the basket or tray of your air fryer.
7. Set the temperature to 390 degrees Fahrenheit and set the time to 5 minutes.
8. At the 2 or 3-minute mark, flip the sandwiches over.
9. Enjoy immediately so the cheese stays hot and melted!

Healthier Fish and Chips

In England and New Zealand, fish and chips are an absolutely classic takeaway dish. Served in newspaper and steaming hot, they are incredibly tasty but incredibly "treat-like". Your air fryer gives you the option to enjoy fish and chips without all the artery-clogging fat. Use any fresh white fish you can source.

Serves: 4
Time: approximately 20 minutes

Ingredients:
- 3 large potatoes, cut into chips (thick-cut fries)
- Oil spray
- Salt and pepper
- 4 fresh white fish filets
- 2 Tbsp. flour
- 1 egg, lightly beaten
- 1 cup breadcrumbs
- Salt and pepper
- Lemon wedges, ketchup and aioli to serve

Method:
1. Give your potato chips a spray with your oil spray and sprinkle with salt and pepper.
2. Pop them into the basket or tray of your air fryer, set the temperature to 390 degrees Fahrenheit and set the time to 30 minutes. OR use the "fries" setting on your air fryer and cook according to the manufacturer's instructions for raw, homemade fries.
3. While the chips are cooking, prep the fish: coat the filets in flour and shake off the excess. Dip them into the beaten egg and let the excess drain off. Dip them into the breadcrumbs and sprinkle with salt and pepper.
4. When the chips have 10 minutes left to cook, place the fish into the air fryer to cook with the chips.
5. Once the fryer beeps, check to ensure the fish and chips are cooked to your liking, and pop them back in for longer if you wish. The fish should be crispy on the outside and moist in the middle, same goes for the chips.
6. Serve with fresh lemon wedges, ketchup and aioli!

Crab Cakes

A simple, fresh and healthy crab cake. You can add extra herbs and spices if you wish, and serve the cakes with your favorite dipping sauces!

Serves: makes approximately 12 crab cakes
Time: approximately 15 minutes (or more if you need to do multiple batches)

Ingredients:
- 1 lb. crab meat, shredded
- 2 eggs, lightly beaten
- ½ cup breadcrumbs
- ⅓ cup finely chopped scallions
- ¼ cup chopped fresh parsley
- 1 heaped Tbsp creamy mayonnaise
- 1 tsp. sweet chili sauce
- ½ tsp. paprika
- Salt and pepper
- Oil spray

Method:
1. Place the crab meat, eggs, breadcrumbs, scallions, parsley, mayonnaise, sweet chili sauce, paprika, salt and pepper into a large bowl and use your hands to combine the mixture thoroughly.
2. Shape the mixture into 12 cakes and give them a light spray with oil spray.
3. You can use baking paper to line the basket or tray of your air fryer if you want to avoid any sticking.
4. Lay the crab cakes onto the basket or tray, careful not to overcrowd. Use multiple layers if your air fryer allows, or else cook the cakes in batches.
5. Set the temperature to 360 degrees Fahrenheit and set the time to 10 minutes.
6. At the 5-minute mark, turn the cakes over.
7. Serve hot, warm or cold with your choice of dipping sauces!

Breaded Scallops

Like most seafood treasures, scallops really don't need a lot of added flavor. This recipe uses a touch of breadcrumbs and some simple seasoning. You can pump up the flavor by serving with a range of tasty dips and sauces, and perhaps a sprinkle of fresh parsley on top.

Serves: makes 16 scallops
Time: approximately 10 minutes

Ingredients:
- 16 fresh scallops
- 3 Tbsp. flour mixed with salt and pepper
- 1 egg, lightly beaten
- 1 cup (give or take) panko crumbs or plain breadcrumbs
- Oil spray

Method:
1. Toss the scallops in the flour and shake off the excess.
2. Dip the scallops into the egg and let the excess drain off.
3. Dip the scallops into the crumbs and ensure they're thoroughly coated.
4. Spray the scallops with oil spray.
5. Line your air fryer basket or rack with baking paper if you'd like to avoid sticking.
6. Lay the scallops in a single layer into your basket or rack.
7. Set the temperature to 390 degrees Fahrenheit and set the time to 5 minutes.
8. At the 2 or 3-minute mark, turn the scallops.
9. Scallops can sometimes leak a bit of fluid after being cooked, so just pop them onto a paper towel until you're ready to serve them, but they're best served right away, perhaps with a creamy dip such as lemon mayonnaise!

Fish Pie

This fish pie recipe is creamy, mild, and has a touch of lemon and herbs. The pastry doesn't encase the whole pie, it is only on the top as a "lid" which makes it slightly healthier and lighter than other pies. You can use any kind of smoked fish you like! Salmon is a rich and tasty choice, while white fish makes a fresh, light pie.

Serves: makes 4 small pies or 1 large pie
Time: approximately 30 minutes

Ingredients:
- 3 Tbsp. butter
- 3 Tbsp. flour
- 1 onion, finely chopped
- 2 garlic cloves, finely chopped
- 2 cups full-fat milk
- Zest of one lemon
- Sprig of fresh thyme, leaves roughly chopped
- Salt and pepper
- 1 lb. smoked fish, flaked
- Store bought pie crust pastry (enough for 4 small pies or 1 large pie)

Method:
1. Prepare your small pie pans or large pie pan by greasing with butter or oil spray, ensure they fit in your air fryer first!
2. Place the butter into a large saucepan over a medium heat until melted.
3. Add the flour to the saucepan and stir into the butter to create a roux.
4. Add the onion and garlic and stir through, let cook for about 2 minutes.
5. Pour the milk into the saucepan and whisk as you do so, so the sauce becomes smooth and lump-free.
6. Keep whisking as the sauce becomes nice and thick.
7. Add the lemon zest, thyme, salt and pepper to taste, stir through.
8. Take the saucepan off the heat and add the fish, stir through.
9. Pour the fish mixture into your pie pan/s and smooth out the top.
10. Place a lid of pastry onto the pie/s and cut a few slits into the top.
11. Place the pie/s into the air fryer and set the temperature to 380 degrees Fahrenheit and the time to 15 minutes.
12. When the timer beeps, check to see that the pastry is golden and flaky.
13. Serve the pie/s nice and hot with a side of buttered veggies!

Chili-lime Salmon and Sesame Broccoli

This recipe combines three incredible flavors: chili, lime and sesame. The salmon is lifted by the vibrancy of the ingredients, while still maintaining that creamy oiliness we know and love. The broccoli is seasoned with soy sauce instead of salt for an extra dimension. An easy but extremely impressive dinner option!

Serves: 2 (date night?!)
Time: approximately 20 minutes

Ingredients:
- 2 fresh salmon filets
- 1 tsp. olive oil
- Juice of 1 lime
- 1 tsp. chili flakes
- Salt and pepper
- 1 head of broccoli, cut into florets
- 1 tsp. sesame oil
- 1 Tbsp. soy sauce

Method:
1. Combine the olive oil, lime juice, chili flakes, salt and pepper in a small bowl or cup.
2. Rub the salmon filets with the oil mixture and massage it into the flesh.
3. Place the broccoli into the air fryer and drizzle the sesame oil over the top.
4. If you have a divider, use it to separate the salmon from the broccoli, otherwise just nestle them in together.
5. Set the time to 350 degrees Fahrenheit and set the time to 8 minutes.
6. Once the timer beeps, check to ensure the salmon is cooked to your liking (I like my salmon to be medium-rare).
7. Drizzle the soy sauce over the broccoli before serving!

Panko-coated Seafood Platter

This is a recipe to turn to when you've got guests coming, or you need to bring a plate of finger food to a party or potluck dinner. Use any fresh seafood and fish you can source!

Serves: makes enough for one medium-large platter
Time: approximately 15 minutes

Ingredients:
- 2 lb. fresh seafood: scallops, mussels, fish filet pieces, prawns, shrimp etc... cleaned as necessary
- 3 eggs, lightly beaten
- Salt and pepper
- 1 cup (might need more) panko breadcrumbs mixed with the zest of 1 lemon
- Oil spray
- Sweet chili sauce, lemon mayonnaise and garlic yogurt for dipping

Method:
1. Prep your seafood by cleaning as needed.
2. Dip each piece of seafood into the beaten egg and let the excess drain off.
3. Sprinkle the seafood with salt and pepper.
4. Roll the seafood in the panko crumbs until coated.
5. Spray the coated seafood with oil spray.
6. Lay the seafood into the basket or tray of your air fryer.
7. Set the temperature to 340 degrees Fahrenheit and set the time to 8 minutes.
8. At the 4-minute mark, turn the seafood.
9. Once the timer beeps, check to ensure the seafood is cooked to your liking.
10. Pile the seafood onto a platter and assemble little bowls of dips and sauces around the platter before serving.

Smoked Fish Quiche

This quiche just needs a store bought pastry crust, some smoked fish, some eggs, herbs and a sprinkling of grated cheese. Wonderful warm or cold, for lunch or dinner.

Serves: makes 1 quiche
Time: approximately 30 minutes

Ingredients:
- 1 store bought quiche pastry case
- 5 eggs, lightly beaten
- 4 Tbsp. heavy cream
- ¼ cup finely chopped scallions
- ¼ cup finely chopped parsley
- 1 tsp. baking powder
- Salt and pepper
- 1 lb. smoked fish
- 1 cup grated cheddar cheese

Method:
1. Place the eggs, cream, scallions, parsley, baking powder, salt and pepper into a large bowl and whisk to combine.
2. Add the fish and cheese, stir to combine.
3. Pour the fish mixture into your pastry case and very carefully place it into the basket or rack of your air fryer, with baking paper beneath to catch any spills.
4. Set the temperature to 390 degrees Fahrenheit and set the time to 20 minutes.
5. At the 12-minute mark, check the quiche to ensure it isn't overcooking.
6. Serve warm or cold, with a tangy tomato relish!

Vegan & Vegetarian

These recipes cater to vegans, vegetarians and anyone who loves and appreciates a meatless meal. You can make many of the vegetarian recipes vegan by omitting or swapping any dairy products i.e. swap halloumi for tofu!

Roasted Veggies with Balsamic Dressing (Vegan and Vegetarian)

Balsamic vinegar and maple syrup gives these veggies a sweet, tangy flavor. Use any veggies you have (apart from leafy or salad veggies). Serve as a side dish or with a poached egg on top for a healthy, easy dinner.

Serves: 4
Time: approximately 30 minutes

Ingredients:
- 2 lb. chopped veggies: use whatever's in season such as potatoes, sweet potatoes, parsnips, zucchini, pumpkin, carrot, leeks etc.
- 2 Tbsp. olive oil
- 1 Tbsp. balsamic vinegar
- 1 Tbsp. maple syrup
- Salt and pepper

Method:
1. Place the olive oil, balsamic vinegar, maple syrup, salt and pepper into a small bowl or cup, whisk with a fork to combine.
2. Place the prepared veggies into your air fryer basket or tray, drizzle the dressing over and combine with your hands until the veggies are all coated.
3. If your air fryer is small, use your discretion and cook the veggies in batches if you feel they're too crowded in one go.
4. Set the temperature to 390 degrees Fahrenheit and set the timer to 20 minutes.
5. At the 10-minute mark, give the veggies a toss or shake.
6. Once the timer beeps, check to ensure the veggies are cooked and tender, pop them back in for a few more minutes if you feel they need a bit longer.
7. Serve warm or hot!

Corn Cakes (Vegetarian)

Crispy, fluffy, tasty corn cakes with sour cream and tomato relish. The perfect weekend brunch or lunch. You can also make mini corn cakes to take as a plate to potluck dinners or BBQ's.

Serves: makes about 12 corn cakes
Time: approximately 25 minutes

Ingredients:

- 3 cups corn kernels (frozen, fresh or canned and drained)
- 3 eggs, lightly beaten
- 1/3 cup finely chopped scallions
- ¼ cup roughly chopped cilantro
- ½ cup self-raising flour
- ½ cup ground almonds (or just use more flour if you don't have ground almonds)
- ½ tsp. baking powder
- Salt and pepper
- Sour cream and tomato relish to serve (just a tasty suggestion!)

Method:

1. Place the corn, eggs, cilantro and scallions into a bowl and stir to combine.
2. Sift the flour, ground almonds and baking powder into the bowl and stir to combine.
3. Add the salt and pepper and stir to combine.
4. Line your air fryer basket or tray with baking paper and place dollops of batter onto the paper, making sure there's at least an inch between the dollops so they can spread.
5. You may need to do multiple batches if your air fryer doesn't have multiple levels.
6. Set the temperature to 380 degrees Fahrenheit and the time to 12 minutes.
7. At the 6-minute mark, turn the cakes and check on their progress to ensure they're not cooking too quickly.
8. Serve hot, warm or cold with tasty toppings such as sour cream, relish and chopped chives!

Baked Potatoes with Cheese and Corn Stuffing (Vegetarian)

Winter or Summer, baked potatoes loaded with cheese, corn, tofu bacon and scallions are the ultimate treat. To make them a bit healthier, you can swap sour cream for Greek yogurt, and halve the amount of cheese.

Serves: makes 2 whole potatoes and 4 halves (1 whole potato per serving)
Time: approximately 1 hour

Ingredients:
- 2 large potatoes (baking variety)
- Oil spray
- Salt and pepper
- 1 cup grated cheddar cheese
- 1 cup corn kernels
- 4 rashers of tofu bacon, fried and chopped (optional)
- 1/3 cup finely chopped scallions
- 2 Tbsp. sour cream

Method:
1. Spray the potatoes with oil spray and rub with salt and pepper.
2. Give them a few pricks with a fork and pop them into your air fryer basket or tray.
3. Set the temperature to 390 degrees Fahrenheit and set the timer to 50 minutes.
4. After 30 minutes, check the potatoes. Different potatoes and different air fryers can cook at faster rates, so just check to see how they're going and judge from there.
5. Once the potatoes are nice and soft, leave them to cool until cool enough to handle.
6. Slice the potatoes in half, lengthways.
7. Scoop the fluffy potato out of the skins and place into a bowl.
8. Add the cheese, corn, tofu bacon, scallions and a pinch more salt and pepper to the bowl, stir to combine.
9. Refill the potato skins with the cheesy filling and sprinkle a little more cheese on top of each one if you wish.
10. Pop them back into the air fryer and cook for 5 minutes at 390 degrees Fahrenheit so the cheese becomes melted.
11. Top with a dollop of sour cream and devour heartily!

Crunchy Fried Tofu (Vegan and Vegetarian)

Cornflakes come in handy once again, this time to give tofu slices a crunchy, golden coating. Serve this tasty tofu as a starter with dipping sauces, pop it in a fresh slaw or serve with rice and veggies for an easy, filling dinner.

Serves: 4
Time: approximately 25 minutes

Ingredients:
- 2 large blocks of firm tofu, cut into even slices about ½ inch thick (no need to be exact about weight, just your standard tofu blocks are fine)
- 2 Tbsp. olive oil
- ½ cup chickpea flour
- ½ cup crushed cornflakes
- Salt and pepper
- Oil spray

Method:
1. Drizzle the olive oil over the tofu strips and rub gently until each strip is coated.
2. Combine the chickpea flour, cornflakes, salt and pepper and lay onto a plate.
3. Dip each tofu strip into the cornflake mixture until coated.
4. Give the coated tofu strips a light spray with oil spray.
5. Line your air fryer basket or tray with baking paper and lay the tofu strips in a single layer onto the paper (do multiple batches if your air fryer is too small to do just one).
6. Set the temperature to 390 degrees Fahrenheit and the time to 12 minutes.
7. At the 6-minute mark, turn the tofu strips.
8. Serve with your favorite vegetarian/vegan dips and sauces.

Veggie Tacos (Vegetarian)

You can opt for soft or hard taco shells, they both work. Personally, I like to use soft flour taco shells most of the time. These tacos are filled with simple, affordable ingredients and are great for weekend dinners and enjoying with a margarita or three.

Serves: 3 (makes 6 tacos, 2 per serving, make more if you need to)
Time: approximately 30 minutes

Ingredients:
- 6 soft taco shells (use hard ones if you prefer)
- 1 cup red kidney beans, drained
- 1 cup black beans, drained
- ½ cup tomato puree
- 1 fresh red chili, finely chopped
- 1 cup fresh cilantro, roughly chopped
- 1 cup corn kernels
- ½ tsp. ground cumin
- ½ tsp. paprika
- Salt and pepper
- 1 cup grated cheese
- Oil spray
- Sour cream and guacamole to serve

Method:
1. Place the kidney beans, black beans, tomato puree, chili, cilantro, corn, cumin, paprika, salt and pepper into into a large bowl and stir to combine.
2. If using soft tacos, place mixture onto one half of the round, sprinkle the cheese over the top and fold the other side over.
3. If using hard taco shells, simply fill them carefully with bean mixture then sprinkle the cheese on top.
4. Spray the air fryer basket or rack with oil spray.
5. Carefully place the filled tacos into the basket or rack.
6. Set the temperature to 390 degrees Fahrenheit and set the time to 12 minutes.
7. Once the timer beeps, check to see that the tacos are hot, bubbling and the cheese has melted.
8. Serve hot with guacamole and sour cream!

Fried Halloumi and Veggies (Vegetarian)

Halloumi cheese and root veggies are a wonderful combination. You can use this recipe as the basis of studier dishes, perhaps with pasta, couscous or quinoa for extra bulk and fiber. Or, you can simply enjoy it as it is for a light meal.

Serves: 2 (as a large meal)
Time: approximately 15 minutes

Ingredients:

- 7 oz. (give or take) block of firm halloumi cheese, cut into cubes
- 2 zucchinis, cut into even chunks
- 1 large carrot, cut into chunks
- 1 large parsnip, cut into chunks
- 2 tsp. olive oil
- 1 tsp. dried mixed herbs
- Salt and pepper

Method:

1. Place the halloumi, zucchini, carrot, parsnip, olive oil, herbs, salt and pepper into a large bowl and gently toss to coat with oil and seasoning.
2. Tip the halloumi and veggies into your air fryer basket or tray. If your air fryer is very small you may need to do multiple batches.
3. Set the temperature to 380 degrees Fahrenheit and set the time to 12 minutes.

Note: if you have a rotating basket, you could use it for this dish if you feel as though your halloumi is firm enough not to break apart

4. When the timer beeps, check to ensure the veggies are tender and the halloumi is golden, pop them back in for a few minutes if they need a bit more time.
5. Enjoy with a drizzle of olive oil and a scattering of fresh arugula leaves!

Tempura Veggies (Vegan and Vegetarian)

Everyone loves a good tempura veggie. Use any veggies you can source, especially harder veggies such as carrots and parsnips. Softer veggies like zucchini and green beans are fine too. The dipping sauce is a suggestion, make your own signature sauce instead if you like! Sometimes I serve these tempura veggies with a pile of sticky rice for a carb-rich, comforting meal.

Serves: 4 as a starter, snack or basis of a rice dish
Time: approximately 20 minutes (depending on how many batches you need to cook the veggies in)

Ingredients:
- 2 lb. sliced mixed veggies for example: carrot, parsnip, sweet potato, green beans, zucchini, onion rings, asparagus, cauliflower
- 1 ½ cups plain flour
- Salt and pepper
- 1 ½ Tbsp. vegan cornstarch
- ¾ cup icy cold water
- Oil spray

Dipping sauce:
- 4 Tbsp. soy sauce
- Juice of 1 lemon
- ½ tsp. sesame oil
- ½ tsp. sugar
- ½ garlic clove, crushed or finely chopped
- ½ tsp. chili sauce (sriracha, sweet chili or anything else you have which packs a little heat)

Method:
1. Line your air fryer basket or tray with baking paper.
2. Prep your veggies by chopping them into even-sized slices.
3. Place the flour, salt, pepper and cornstarch into a large bowl and whisk to combine.
4. Keep whisking as you pour the iced water into the dry ingredients until a smooth batter forms.
5. Dip each piece of vegetable into the batter and let the excess drip away, put the battered veggies straight into your air fryer basket or tray, lined with baking paper.

6. Secure the basket or tray into the air fryer and set the temperature to 390 degrees Fahrenheit and the time to 10 minutes.
7. At the 5-minute mark, turn the veggies over.
8. When the timer beeps, check to ensure the veggies are really crispy and pop them back in for a few minutes if need be.
9. Make your dipping sauce by combining all ingredients in a small bowl.

Note: you may need to do multiple batches if your air fryer doesn't have multiple layers.

Air-fried Falafels (Vegan and Vegetarian)

Falafels are not just for vegans and vegetarians, EVERYONE loves them... or should love them at least. They're like little patties of goodness which happen to be incredibly moreish and satisfying. Sometimes I serve a big platter of them with toothpicks and a couple of dipping sauces. Other times I pop them into warm pita breads with fresh salad and tahini... the world's your falafel.

Serves: makes approximately 20 falafels (4 or 5 per serving)
Time: approximately 25 minutes

Ingredients:
- 2 cups cooked chickpeas (I don't bother with dried chickpeas, I just use the canned ones)
- ½ cup chickpea flour (or any other flour you have or prefer)
- 1 cup fresh parsley, finely chopped
- Juice of 1 lemon
- 5 garlic cloves, roughly chopped
- 1 brown onion, roughly chopped
- 2 tsp. ground cumin
- 2 tsp. ground coriander
- 1 tsp. chili powder
- ½ tsp. turmeric (optional: I love the colour it gives the falafel)
- Salt and pepper (pop a generous pinch of salt in and taste the mixture to ensure it's well seasoned)
- Oil spray

Method:
1. Put the chickpeas, chickpea flour, parsley, lemon juice, garlic, onion, cumin, coriander, chili, turmeric, salt and pepper into a food processor, pulse until the mixture is combined but not too battery, there should still be little bits of rice-sized chickpeas in the mixture.
2. Roll the mixture into approximately 20 balls and gently flatten them with your hand, but ensure they're still quite round (i.e. not like a burger patty).
3. Give them a spray with oil spray and lay them onto a paper-lined air fryer basket or tray.

Note: do multiple batches if your air fryer isn't large enough to do one batch without crowding or layering the falafel.

4. Set the temperature to 390 degrees Fahrenheit and set the time to 12 minutes.

5. At the 6-minute mark, carefully turn the falafels over.
6. Once the timer beeps, check to ensure the falafels are crunchy and deep golden, pop them back in for a few more minutes if you feel they need more time to cook.
7. Serve however you fancy!

Fried Polenta Fries (Vegetarian - can be made Vegan)

Polenta fries can be found on trendy menus all around the world these days and for good reason, they're incredibly satisfying to munch on. With a crunchy outer and a dense inner, they're an ideal snack as you enjoy a glass of wine on a Summer's night, or as an impressive starter at dinner parties.

Serves: approximately 4

Time: approximately 90 minutes (including refrigeration time to set the polenta)

Ingredients:
- 2 cups water
- 2 cups full-fat milk (substitute for water for a vegan option)
- 1 cup instant polenta
- Salt and pepper
- Oil spray
- Fresh thyme, roughly chopped

Method:
1. Prepare a baking tray with baking paper - doesn't need to fit in the air fryer, it's just for cooling and setting the polenta in the fridge.
2. Pour the water and milk into a saucepan and bring to a simmer.
3. Use a whisk to keep the mixture moving as you pour the polenta into the liquid.
4. Keep whisking as the polenta becomes thick and bubbling.
5. Season with salt and pepper.
6. Pour the polenta into your lined baking tray and spread out, place it into the fridge until cold and set.
7. Slice the cold, set polenta into batons (like thick-cut fries) and spray them with oil spray.
8. Lay the polenta chips into your air fryer basket or rack (do multiple layers if your air fryer allows, or you may have to do multiple batches to avoid overcrowding the air fryer).
9. Set the temperature to 390 degrees Fahrenheit and set the time to 15 minutes.
10. At the 7 or 8-minute mark, turn the polenta fries.
11. When the timer beeps, ensure the fries are crispy and golden, pop them back in if they require more cooking.
12. Serve with your favorite vegan or vegetarian dipping sauces!

Fried Veggie Sushi (Vegan and Vegetarian)

Sushi is great, but FRIED sushi is even better. These rolls are filled with super simple ingredients: carrot, avocado and bell pepper. You can add any other fillings you like best.

Serves: approximately 4

Time: approximately 1 hour (including cooking and cooling the rice and rolling the sushi)

Ingredients:

- 2 cups cooked sushi rice, (cook according to packet directions or use your go-to method)
- 4 nori sheets (sushi seaweed)
- 1 carrot, finely sliced lengthways
- 1 red bell pepper, seeds removed, thinly sliced
- 1 avocado, sliced
- 1 Tbsp. olive oil mixed with 1 Tbsp rice wine vinegar
- 1 cup panko crumbs
- 2 Tbsp. sesame seeds
- Oil spray
- Soy sauce, wasabi and pickled ginger to serve

Method:

1. Get a clean board, a small bowl of warm water and a sushi mat (if you have one) ready.
2. Lay a nori sheet onto your sushi mat and spread ½ cup sushi rice onto it, leaving ½ an inch of nori clear so you can use it to seal the sushi roll. Wet hands make spreading the sushi rice a bit easier.
3. Place the carrot, bell pepper and avocado along the width of the rice.
4. Tightly roll your sushi and rub warm water along the clean nori strip to seal the roll (if you're a sushi newbie, there are SO many sushi rolling tutorials online, so make use of them!).
5. Have your olive oil and rice wine vinegar mixture ready in a bowl nearby.
6. Mix the panko crumbs with the sesame seeds in a large bowl and place next to the oil/vinegar bowl.
7. Roll each sushi log in the oil/vinegar and transfer straight to the panko/sesame seed bowl and thoroughly coat.
8. Place the coated sushi logs into your air fryer basket or tray and set the

    temperature to 390 degrees Fahrenheit and the time to 12 minutes.
9. At the 6-minute mark, give the rolls a turn.
10. Once the air fryer beeps, ensure that the sushi logs are golden and crispy on the outside.
11. Slice the logs into pieces and serve with soy sauce, pickled ginger and wasabi.

Teriyaki Cauliflower (Vegan and Vegetarian)

Cauliflower takes on any flavor it is dressed with, and this teriyaki sauce has a fantastic flavor. It's sweet, salty, sticky and has a little touch of heat. Serve with rice, edamame beans and an extra drizzle of soy sauce.

Serves: 4 (as a meal served with either rice or noodles)
Time: approximately 20 minutes

Ingredients:

- 2 small cauliflower heads or one very large one, cut into florets
- ½ cup soy sauce
- 4 Tbsp. brown sugar
- 1 tsp. sesame oil
- 1/3 cup water
- ½ chili powder
- 2 cloves garlic, finely chopped
- 1 tsp. cornstarch

Method:

1. Place the soy sauce, brown sugar, sesame oil, water, chili powder, garlic and cornstarch into a measuring cup and whisk with a fork until smooth and combined.
2. Place the cauliflower into a large bowl and pour the teriyaki sauce over the top, toss with your hands or a wooden spoon until the cauliflower is coated.
3. Place the cauliflower into the basket or rack of your air fryer.
4. Set the temperature to 380 degrees Fahrenheit and the time to 12 minutes.
5. At the 6-mark, give the cauliflower a gentle shake or toss.
6. Once the timer beeps, check to ensure the cauliflower is cooked but not too soft.
7. Serve with rice and edamame beans!

Breakfast

Some of these breakfast recipes are really light and healthy, but many of them are absolutely decadent. A great mix of recipes for weekday mornings, weekend brunches and even a celebratory champagne breakfast.

Banana Bread

Banana bread, what else can I say? If you want to make this even more decadent you can add chocolate chips. Eat warm with butter, or place onto the grill and top with vanilla ice cream and caramel sauce for an extra-special breakfast-dessert.

Serves: makes 1 loaf (8-12 slices depending on thickness)
Time: approximately 1 hour

Ingredients:
- ½ cup melted butter
- 1 egg, lightly beaten
- ½ cup brown sugar
- 1 tsp. vanilla extract
- 3 ripe bananas, mashed
- 1 ½ cups plain flour
- 1 tsp. baking powder
- ½ tsp. grated nutmeg
- ½ tsp. ground cinnamon
- Butter, to serve

Method:
1. Prepare a loaf tin by spraying with oil spray and lining with baking paper, ensure it fits into your air fryer.
2. Place the melted butter, egg, brown sugar, vanilla and bananas into a large bowl and whisk to combine.
3. Sift the flour, baking powder, nutmeg and cinnamon into the bowl and stir to combine but don't overmix.
4. Pour the batter into your prepared tin and pop it into your air fryer.
5. Set the temperature to 330 degrees Fahrenheit and set the time to 30 minutes.
6. At the 20-minute mark, check the banana bread to see how it's coming along, all air fryers are different and yours may cook faster than others. Judge the rest of the cooking time from there.
7. When the timer beeps, carefully take the loaf pan out of the air fryer and leave to cool before turning it out, slicing and slathering each slice with butter!

Hash Browns

This is one big hash brown as opposed to lots of little ones, it's just easier that way. You can slice it into wedges, squares, or any shape you like. It has onions, garlic and cheese for extra flavor in the morning.

Serves: makes 1 large hash brown which can be sliced into about 4 servings
Time: approximately 25 minutes

Ingredients:
- 4 potatoes (agria or russet are great), peeled and grated
- 1 brown onion, finely chopped
- 4 garlic cloves, finely chopped
- ½ cup grated cheddar cheese
- 1 egg, lightly beaten
- Salt and pepper
- 3 Tbsp. finely chopped chives
- Oil spray

Method:
1. Place the grated potato into a muslin cloth or thin tea towel and squeeze to remove the moisture.
2. Place the squeezed potato into a large bowl and add the onion, garlic, cheese, egg, salt, pepper and chives, combine with your hands or a wooden spoon.
3. Spray your air fryer basket or tray with oil spray.
4. Press the hash brown mixture into your basket or tray and place it back into the air fryer.
5. Set the temperature to 380 degrees Fahrenheit and the time to 10 minutes.
6. Once the timer beeps, ensure the hash brown is golden and crispy on the outside and cooked through.
7. Serve with poached eggs and bacon!

Bacon and Egg Muffins

These muffins are perfect for people with gluten intolerances as they don't contain any flour. In fact, they're really healthy! You can store them in the fridge and grab a couple for a really quick, no-mess breakfast.

Serves: makes 12 muffins
Time: approximately 30 minutes

Ingredients:
- 12 eggs, lightly beaten
- 10 bacon rashers, cut into small pieces
- ½ cup finely chopped chives
- 1 brown onion, finely chopped
- 1 cup grated cheddar cheese
- Salt and pepper
- Oil spray

Method:
1. Prepare a 12-hole muffin pan (or any muffin pan which fits into your air fryer) by spraying with oil spray.
2. Place the eggs, bacon, chives, onion, cheese, salt and pepper into a large pourable measuring bowl and stir to combine.
3. Pour the batter into muffin pans and place into the air fryer.
4. Set the temperature to 360 degrees Fahrenheit and set the temperature to 10 minutes.
5. Once the timer beeps, check to ensure the muffins are set, if not, pop them back in for a few more minutes.
6. Serve with toasted, buttered ciabatta on the side (just an idea!).

Breakfast Berry Oat Bars

Oats in the morning don't always need to come in the form of oatmeal. They can be baked into a delicious bar like this one, with berries nestled inside. If your air fryer doesn't fit a traybake pan you can make this recipe into muffins instead.

Serves: makes approximately 12 bars
Time: approximately 40 minutes

Ingredients:
- 3 cups rolled oats
- ½ cup ground almonds
- ½ cup flour
- 1 tsp. baking powder
- 1 tsp. ground cinnamon
- 3 eggs, lightly beaten
- ½ cup coconut or canola oil
- 1/3 cup milk
- 2 tsp. vanilla extract
- 2 cups mixed berries (or one berry, your favorite one)

Method:
1. Prepare a traybake pan (ensure it fits into your air fryer) by spraying with oil spray.
2. Place the oats, ground almonds, flour, baking powder and cinnamon into a large bowl and stir to combine.
3. In a smaller bowl, whisk together the eggs, oil, milk and vanilla.
4. Stir the wet ingredients into the oat mixture until gently combined.
5. Fold the berries into the mixture.
6. Pour the mixture into the prepared pan and place into your air fryer.
7. Set the temperature to 370 degrees Fahrenheit and set the time to 25 minutes.
8. Once the timer beeps, check to ensure the bars are cooked through. They may still be a bit raw so just pop them back in until they gently spring back but are still nice and soft.
9. Serve warm or cold, with a dollop of thick Greek yogurt on top!

Spinach, Mushroom and Feta Omelet

An egg-based breakfast with spinach, mushrooms and feta. Great for vegetarians and those on a low-carb eating plan.

Serves: makes 1 omelet, enough for 2 people
Time: approximately 10 minutes

Ingredients:
- 4 eggs, lightly beaten
- 3 Tbsp. heavy cream
- 2 cups spinach, roughly chopped
- 1 cup chopped mushrooms
- 4 oz. feta cheese, crumbled or chopped
- Handful of fresh parsley, finely chopped
- Salt and pepper
- Oil spray

Method:
1. Prepare your air fryer basket or a shallow pan (depending on your air fryer) by spraying with oil spray.
2. Place the eggs and cream into a bowl and whisk together until combined.
3. Add the spinach, mushrooms, feta, parsley, salt and pepper and stir to combine.
4. Pour the mixture into the air fryer basket or pan and secure into the air fryer.
5. Set the temperature to 360 degrees Fahrenheit and set the time to 5 minutes.
6. Once the timer beeps, check to ensure the omelet is just set but still a bit wobbly.
7. Serve hot, warm or cold! A touch of tangy tomato relish on the side doesn't go astray!

Banana, Walnut and Chocolate Muffins

Banana and walnuts - one of the best breakfast combinations. I've added chocolate because I love it, but you can leave it out if you'd prefer not to have chocolate at breakfast time.

Serves: makes 12 muffins
Time: approximately 40 minutes

Ingredients:
- ½ cup melted butter
- ½ cup honey
- 2 eggs, lightly beaten
- 4 ripe bananas, mashed
- 1 tsp. vanilla extract
- 2 cups plain or whole wheat flour
- 1 tsp. baking powder
- ½ tsp. baking soda
- 1 tsp. ground cinnamon
- ½ cup chopped walnuts
- ½ cup dark chocolate chips

Method:
1. Prepare a 12-hole muffin pan by spraying with oil spray or lining with cupcake cases.
2. Place the butter, honey, eggs, banana and vanilla into a large bowl and whisk to combine.
3. Sift the flour, baking powder, baking soda and cinnamon into the bowl fold into the wet ingredients without overmixing.
4. Fold the walnuts and chocolate into the mixture.
5. Spoon the mixture into the prepared muffin holes and pop into the air fryer.
6. Set the temperature to 360 degrees Fahrenheit and set the time to 30 minutes.
7. At the 20-minute mark, check the muffins to ensure they aren't cooking too quickly, (again all air fryers are different and yours might be speedy and hot!).
8. Once the timer beeps, take the muffin pan out of the air fryer and leave to cool before turning the muffins out onto a board.
9. Serve warm or cold, with a scraping of butter!

Caramel-filled French Toast

Yes, these are very decadent and not healthy at all. But hey, this isn't a diet book! Have a healthy, light omelet during the week then dig into some of these luxurious morsels of french toast and caramel on Saturday morning.

Serves: 4
Time: approximately 15 minutes

Ingredients:
- 8 slices brioche or white bread
- 2 eggs
- ¼ cup heavy cream
- 1/3 cup caster (superfine) sugar mixed with 1 tsp ground cinnamon
- 8 Tbsp. store bought or homemade caramel
- Oil spray

Method:
1. Whisk together the eggs and cream in a small bowl.
2. Dip each piece of brioche into the egg and cream, allowing the excess to drip away.
3. Dip the bread into the sugar and cinnamon mixture until each side is coated.
4. Lay the coated slices onto a board and spread FOUR of the slices with 2 Tbsp caramel each. Don't spread it right to the sides, keep it nearer the middle to prevent it from oozing out into the air fryer.
5. Place the remaining four slices on top to create four sandwiches.
6. Spray the basket or tray of your air fryer with oil spray.
7. Lay the sandwiches into the basket or tray and secure into the air fryer unit.
8. Set the temperature to 360 degrees Fahrenheit and set the time to 8 minutes.
9. At the 4-minute mark, turn the sandwiches over.
10. Once the timer beeps, carefully remove the sandwiches from the air fryer with tongs, they'll be hot!
11. Serve with cream, yogurt and/or berries.

Ham, Spinach and Mozzarella Fried Sourdough Sandwiches

Sourdough is a beautiful bread for making grilled or fried sandwiches. Ham, spinach and mozzarella melt together for a hot and tasty breakfast or brunch.

Serves: 2
Time: approximately 25 minutes

Ingredients:
- 4 slices sourdough bread
- 2 Tbsp. full-fat mayonnaise
- 2 thick slices of ham
- 2 small handfuls of spinach, enough to fill 2 sandwiches
- 1 tomato, sliced
- 2 large slices of mozzarella cheese, enough to fill 2 sandwiches
- Salt and pepper
- Oil spray

Method:
1. Place the sourdough slices onto clean board and spread each one with mayonnaise.
2. Layer the ham, spinach, tomato and mozzarella onto TWO of the slices.
3. Sprinkle with salt and pepper.
4. Place the remaining two slices on top to create two sandwiches.
5. Spray both sides of the sandwiches with oil spray.
6. Place them into your air fryer basket or tray and secure it into the air fryer unit.
7. Set the temperature to 370 degrees Fahrenheit and set the time to 12 minutes.
8. At the 6-minute mark, flip the sandwiches over.
9. When the timer beeps, remove the sandwiches from the fryer, slice in half and serve immediately so the cheese remains hot and melted when you eat!

Sweet Potato, Spinach and Cheddar Frittata

More spinach, more cheese! Some of the best breakfast ingredients. This frittata uses sweet potatoes and fresh herbs for a fresh alternative to the usual white potato frittata.

Serves: 4

Time: approximately 40 minutes (including time to precook the sweet potatoes)

Ingredients:
- 3 cups sweet potato cubes, steamed or gently boiled until just soft
- 2 cups spinach, roughly chopped
- 6 eggs, lightly beaten
- ¼ cup heavy cream
- 1 cup grated cheddar
- ½ cup parsley, finely chopped
- Few sprigs of fresh thyme, finely chopped
- Salt and pepper

Method:
1. Prepare your air fryer basket or a cake pan (one which fits into your air fryer) by spraying with oil spray.
2. Layer the sweet potatoes into the basket or pan.
3. Whisk together the eggs, cream, spinach, cheddar, parsley, thyme, salt and pepper and pour over the sweet potatoes.
4. Place the basket or pan into the air fryer, set the temperature to 370 degrees Fahrenheit and set the time to 20 minutes.
5. Once the timer beeps, check to ensure that the frittata is set and golden.
6. Serve hot, warm or cold!

Apricot and Almond Scones

There's nothing quite like a warm scone with a knob of butter melting across the soft surface in the morning. These scones have almonds and dried apricots for crunch, chewiness and sweetness.

Serves: makes 12 scones
Time: approximately 30 minutes

Ingredients:
- 2 cups flour
- 1/3 cup sugar
- 2 tsp. baking powder
- ½ cup sliced almonds
- ¾ cup chopped dried apricots
- ¼ cup cold butter, cut into cubes
- ½ cup milk, cream or buttermilk (they all work fine so use what you've got in the fridge)
- 1 egg
- 1 tsp. vanilla extract

Method:
1. Prepare your air fryer basket or tray by lining with baking paper.
2. Stir together the flour, sugar, baking powder, almonds and apricots.
3. Rub the butter into the dry ingredients with your fingers until it resembles a sandy, crumbly texture.
4. Whisk together the milk, egg and vanilla extract.
5. Pour the milk mixture into the dry ingredients and stir together until just combined.
6. Flour a board, turn the dough onto the board and give it a few quick kneads.
7. Shape the dough into a rectangle and cut into 12 squares.
8. Lay the squares onto the basket or tray and pop into the air fryer.
9. Set the temperature to 370 degrees Fahrenheit and set the time to 15 minutes.
10. When the timer beeps, check to ensure that the scones are cooked through, if they need more cooking just put them back in for a few more minutes until done.
11. Serve warm with butter!

Note: if you want to serve these as more of a morning tea treat, a citrusy glaze made from powdered sugar and lemon juice is a nice touch.

Pancetta-wrapped Asparagus Tarts

These could double as appetizers, but to me they are the perfect breakfast for when you want to be a little more impressive than cereal or toast. Great for a champagne breakfast or breakfast date. You will need 6 individual 4-inch tart pans for this recipe.

Serves: makes 6 tarts
Time: approximately 30 minutes

Ingredients:
- Store bought pie pastry, enough for 6 4-inch tarts
- 12 eggs
- ½ cup heavy cream
- ¼ cup finely grated parmesan cheese
- Salt and pepper
- 24 asparagus spears, (woody ends removed), cut in half
- 12 pancetta rashers, cut in half widthways

Method:
1. Prepare your tart pans by thoroughly greasing with butter or oil spray.
2. Line each tart pan with pastry and prick with a fork.
3. Place the lined tarts into the air fryer and cook for 4 minutes at 380 degrees Fahrenheit or until the pastry is just beginning to turn golden.
4. Take the tart pans out of the air fryer and set aside.
5. In a bowl, whisk together the eggs, cream, salt, pepper and parmesan cheese.
6. Wrap each asparagus spear with a piece pancetta.
7. Pour the egg mixture into the pastry-lined tart pans.
8. Lay 4 pancetta-wrapped asparagus pieces into each tart.
9. Carefully place the tarts into your air fryer basket or tray.
10. Set the temperature to 390 degrees Fahrenheit and set the time to 15 minutes.
11. Once the timer beeps, check the tarts to ensure they're just set but not overdone.
12. Serve warm with a side of sourdough and a big pot of HOT coffee (or a mimosa).

Appetizers

Now we come to our appetizer section. Nibbles, finger food and starters fit for dinner parties, game nights, kids' sleepovers or even fancy events which require "a plate" to be supplied by the guests. You can even whip these up as snacks any time, any day!

Garlic and Herb Potato Chips

Potato chips... if there's a bowl of them at a party, that's where I will hang out. Especially if they are amazing, homemade, gourmet potato chips like these ones! Garlic, herbs and simple seasoning create the most special, crunchy chips ever.

Serves: makes 1 large bowl of chips
Time: approximately 1 hour (including soaking time for the potatoes)

Ingredients:

- 4 large potatoes (russet potatoes are good)
- 2 Tbsp. olive oil
- 4 garlic cloves, crushed
- 1 tsp. each of fresh rosemary, thyme and oregano, finely chopped
- Salt and pepper

Method:

1. Using a mandolin or some great knife skills, slice the potatoes as thinly as you can (just imagine your favorite potato chips and slice according to those).
2. Pop the sliced potatoes into a bowl of water with a dash of salt for seasoning, leave for at least 20 minutes and up to 30 minutes. This removes some of the starch from the potatoes. Starch is a sticky substance which reduces the crunchiness of the chips.
3. Rinse and dry the soaked potatoes and return them to the dried bowl.
4. Add the olive oil, garlic, herbs, salt and pepper to the bowl and toss with your hands until all of the potato slices are coated.
5. Lay the potato slices onto your prepared trays or basket and secure into the air fryer.
6. Set the temperature at 360 degrees Fahrenheit and set the time to 15 minutes.
7. Every 5 or so minutes, give the chips a little turn or shake.
8. Once the timer beeps, assess the chips to see if they're golden and crunchy, if not, place them back in for a few more minutes.
9. Serve with onion dip!

Air-fried Croquettes

Cheesy, herby, crispy rice croquettes. Use any kind of white rice you have lying around and remember to season it well when you pre-cook it!

Serves: makes approximately 12 croquettes
Time: approximately 45 minutes (including time to pre-cook the rice)

Ingredients:
- 2 cups cooked rice
- 1 brown onion, finely chopped
- 2 garlic cloves, finely chopped
- 2 eggs, lightly beaten
- ½ cup finely grated parmesan cheese
- Salt and pepper
- ½ cup breadcrumbs
- 1 tsp. dried mixed herbs
- Oil spray

Method:
1. Mix together the rice, onion, garlic, eggs, parmesan, salt and pepper.
2. Shape into 12 croquettes (rounded rectangles).
3. Spread the breadcrumbs onto a plate and roll each croquette in the crumbs until coated.
4. Spray each croquette with oil spray.
5. Lay the croquettes into your air fryer basket or tray.
6. Set the temperature to 390 degrees Fahrenheit and the time to 15 minutes.
7. At the 7 or 8-minute mark, turn the croquettes.
8. Once the timer beeps, check to ensure the croquettes are golden and crispy, if not, pop them back in for a few minutes.
9. Serve with plum sauce or a tangy relish.

Stuffed Mushrooms with Cheese and Red Rice

Red rice gives a chewy, nutty flavor to these cheesy stuffed mushrooms. You can experiment with different herbs and spices if you feel confident!

Serves: makes 12 medium-sized mushrooms
Time: approximately 30 minutes

Ingredients:
- 12 Swiss brown mushrooms
- Olive oil to brush onto the mushrooms
- 1 cup cooked red rice
- 1 cup grated parmesan cheese
- 1 tsp. dried mixed herbs
- Salt and pepper

Method:
1. Brush each mushroom with olive oil and set out onto a board.
2. In a small bowl, combine the cooked red rice, parmesan, herbs, salt and pepper.
3. Stuff each mushroom with the rice mixture, (press a spoonful of mixture onto the mushroom and press down. It can resemble a little mound, it doesn't need to be flat).
4. Lay the mushrooms into your air fryer basket or tray.
5. Set the temperature to 370 degrees Fahrenheit and set the time to 15 minutes.
6. Once the timer beeps, check to ensure the mushrooms are cooked and golden and the cheese has melted into the rice.
7. Serve on a platter with some fresh herbs scattered about.

Smoked Fish Balls

Another appetizer recipe which utilizes the starchy goodness of cooked rice. I find that at dinner parties, guests like snacks and appetizers which have a bit of bulk to them by way of carbs. It holds off hunger until the main course and soaks up the glasses of wine which are undoubtedly being drunk freely!

Serves: makes approximately 16 balls
Time: approximately 50 minutes (including the time to pre-cook the rice)

Ingredients:
- 1 cup smoked fish, any kind, flaked
- 2 cups cooked white, red or brown rice
- 2 eggs, lightly beaten
- 1 cup grated parmesan
- ¼ cup finely chopped thyme
- Salt and pepper
- 1 cup panko crumbs
- Oil spray

Method:
1. Place the fish, rice, eggs, parmesan, thyme, salt and pepper into a bowl and stir to combine.
2. Roll the mixture into 16 even-sized balls.
3. Roll the balls in the breadcrumbs then spray each one with oil spray.
4. Place the balls into your air fryer basket or tray.
5. Set the temperature to 370 degrees Fahrenheit and set the time to 20 minutes.
6. Once the timer beeps, check to ensure the balls are golden and crispy.
7. Serve with any sauce or dip you fancy! A little cup of toothpicks is handy too.

Spring Rolls

These crunchy spring rolls are vegetarian and full of yummy produce. This recipe does take a little more work and a few more dirty dishes as you need to cook the veggies first... but it's worth it for an impressive appetizer.

Serves: makes 12 spring rolls
Time: approximately 30 minutes (including time to pre-cook the vermicelli noodles)

Ingredients:
- 12 small spring roll wrappers
- 1 ½ cups cooked and cooled vermicelli noodles
- 3 garlic cloves, finely chopped
- 1 Tbsp. minced fresh ginger
- 2 Tbsp. soy sauce
- 1 tsp. sesame oil
- 1 yellow bell pepper, seeds removed, finely chopped
- 1 cup finely chopped mushrooms
- 1 cup finely chopped carrot
- ½ cup finely chopped scallions
- Oil spray

Method:
1. Place the garlic, ginger, soy sauce, bell pepper, mushroom, carrot and scallions into a saucepan over a medium heat and stir as they combine, cook and soften.
2. Stir the vermicelli noodles into the cooked veggies and take the pan off the heat.
3. Lay the spring roll wrappers onto a clean board.
4. Place dollops of veggie and noodle mixture onto the center of each spring roll wrapper.
5. Roll the spring rolls and tuck the corners and edges in to create neat and secure rolls.
6. Give the rolls a spray with oil spray and place them into your air fryer basket or tray.
7. Set the temperature to 350 degrees Fahrenheit and set the time to 10 minutes.
8. At the 5-minute mark, give the rolls a gentle shake or turn, check to ensure they're not cooking too quickly.
9. Once the timer beeps, the spring rolls should be golden and crispy.
10. Serve with sweet chili sauce or soy sauce!

Meatballs

Meatballs aren't the prettiest or most glamorous appetizers in the world, but I guarantee you, if you put a platter of them out, they'll be devoured immediately. Serve with toothpicks and dipping sauces.

Serves: makes approximately 30 meatballs
Time: approximately 30 minutes

Ingredients:
- 1 lb. ground beef
- 1 onion, finely chopped
- 3 garlic cloves, finely chopped
- 2 eggs
- 1 cup breadcrumbs
- ½ cup fresh herbs, finely chopped: oregano, mint, thyme, rosemary
- Salt and pepper
- Oil spray

Method:
1. Place the beef, onion, garlic, eggs, breadcrumbs, herbs, salt and pepper into a large bowl and combine with your hands.
2. Roll into even-sized balls and lay onto your air fryer basket or tray.
3. Spray with oil spray.
4. Set the temperature to 390 degrees Fahrenheit and the time to 15 minutes.
5. At the 8-minute mark, turn the meatballs.
6. Once the timer beeps, check to ensure the meatballs are cooked and golden, pop them back in for longer if you feel they're not quite done.
7. Serve with toothpicks and a choice of dips such as lemon aioli, garlic mayo and ketchup.

Pita Pizzas

These mini pizzas made with pita breads have a childlike, nostalgic feel to them. Kids love these as much as adults, so they're great for dinner parties where kids are invited! You can play around with different toppings if you wish.

Serves: makes 6 pita pizzas but they can be cut into wedges to serve more people as an appetizer

Time: approximately 20 minutes

Ingredients:
- 6 pita breads
- 6 Tbsp. marinara sauce (store bought is completely fine)
- 12 rounds of hot salami
- 12 button mushrooms, sliced
- 18 fresh basil leaves
- 2 cups grated mozzarella cheese
- 1 tsp. chili flakes
- Oil spray

Method:
1. Lay the pita breads onto a clean board and give them a spray with oil spray.
2. Spread the marinara sauce over the pita breads.
3. Arrange the salami, mushrooms, basil, mozzarella and chili flakes onto the pizzas.
4. Place the pizzas into your air fryer basket or tray.
5. Set the temperature to 370 degrees Fahrenheit and set the time to 12 minutes.
6. Check on the pizzas halfway through the cooking time to ensure they're not overcooking.
7. When the timer beeps, carefully take the pizzas out of the air fryer and slice into quarters.
8. Serve on a platter with napkins... easy as that!

Spicy Fries

I couldn't go much further without another fried potato recipe! These fries are spicy, smoky and great for dipping into mayo or aioli. Pop a bowl of these hot fries onto the table at any party, game night or get together and your friends will be forever in awe of you and your tasty offerings.

Serves: makes 1 large bowl of fries
Time: approximately 25 minutes (or longer if you need to do multiple batches)

Ingredients:

- 3 large potatoes, (russet potatoes are good for fries)
- 2 tsp. olive oil
- 2 tsp. chili powder
- 1 tsp. paprika
- Salt and pepper

Method:

1. Chop your potatoes into thin fries, rinse in a colander, then dry off with a tea towel.
2. Place the potato fries into a bowl and add the olive oil, chili powder, paprika, salt and pepper.
3. Toss the potatoes with your hands until they're all thoroughly coated in oil and seasoning.
4. If you have a rotating basket with your air fryer you can and should use that, otherwise, load the fries into the basket or tray. If your air fryer is too small to fit the fries comfortably without overcrowding, you may need to do multiple batches.
5. Set the temperature to 380 degrees Fahrenheit and set the timer to 15 minutes.
6. If you're not using a rotating basket, give the fries a toss or shake halfway.
7. Once the timer beeps, check to ensure the fries are golden and crispy.
8. Serve hot, with sauces and dips.

Note: feel free to use the "fries" preset button on your air fryer if it has one.

Cheese and Olive Bruschetta

When French baguettes get a little bit stale, perhaps after a day or two of being baked, they make delicious bruschetta. Of course, you can use fresh bread but the point is that you can avoid wasting older bread as well. Cheese and olives make a simple, salty and tasty topping.

Serves: makes 12 pieces of bruschetta
Time: approximately 25 minutes

Ingredients:
- 12 slices of french baguette
- Olive oil to brush onto the bread
- 4 garlic cloves, minced
- 1 cup grated cheese, use any you prefer but I generally use cheddar or a mix of cheddar and mozzarella
- 12 green olives, sliced
- 1 tsp. dried oregano
- Salt and pepper

Method:
1. Brush the bread slices with olive oil and sprinkle each one with minced garlic.
2. Sprinkle the grated cheese onto the bread, followed by the olives, oregano, salt and pepper.
3. Carefully place the bruschetta into the air fryer basket or tray.
4. Set the temperature to 380 degrees Fahrenheit and set the timer to 12 minutes.
5. At the 7-minute mark, check to ensure the bruschetta are not cooking too quickly.
6. Once the air fryer beeps, take the bruschetta out of the air fryer and place onto a platter, cut them in half if you wish!
7. Serve warm with a scattering of fresh arugula and a drizzle of olive oil (if you like).

Fried Ravioli

This is one of those recipes where the method is so easy and the ingredients list is so short... but the result is unusual, exciting and so tasty. Buy fresh ravioli - the cheaper, packaged ravioli from the supermarket works just fine. This is another appetizer which kids really adore.

Serves: makes 1 large platter of fried ravioli, enough for about 6 people as an appetizer
Time: approximately 25 minutes

Ingredients:
- 2 packages of fresh ravioli, any fillings will do
- 1 cup flour, mixed with salt and pepper
- 3 eggs, lightly beaten
- 1 ½ cups panko or breadcrumbs (you might need a little more)
- Oil spray

Method:
1. Dip the ravioli into the flour and shake off the excess.
2. Dip the ravioli into the beaten egg and let the excess drip away.
3. Dip the ravioli into the breadcrumbs or panko crumbs until coated.
4. Spray the coated ravioli with a light coating of oil spray.
5. Place the ravioli into your air fryer basket or tray in a single layer, you might need to do multiple batches.
6. Set the temperature to 380 degrees Fahrenheit and set the time to 15 minutes.
7. At the 8-minute mark, turn the ravioli.
8. Once the air fryer beeps, ensure the ravioli are golden and fried, pop them back in for a few minutes if you feel they need more cooking time.
9. Serve with dipping sauces: a tangy one such as marinara and a creamy one such as alfredo sauce are great choices.

Goat Cheese, Prune and Bacon Bombs

These "bombs" feature goat cheese, prunes and bacon. They're great for gluten free guests and should be served with toothpicks for easy eating. This is a large recipe so feel free to halve it if you don't need that many.

Serves: makes approximately 30 - 40 bombs
Time: approximately 25 minutes

Ingredients:
- 17 oz. soft goat cheese
- 2 Tbsp. fresh rosemary, finely chopped
- 1 cup almonds, chopped into small pieces
- Salt and pepper
- 20 prunes, chopped
- 30 bacon rashers

Method:
1. Line your air fryer basket or tray with baking paper.
2. Place the goat cheese, rosemary, almonds, salt, pepper and prunes into a large bowl and stir to combine. It might take a bit of elbow grease to combine the ingredients as the goat cheese is extremely thick.
3. Roll the mixture into balls and wrap each one with a bacon rasher.
4. Place the bombs onto a paper-lined basket or tray and secure into the air fryer.
5. Set the temperature to 370 degrees Fahrenheit and set the time to 12 minutes.
6. Check on the bombs after 6 minutes to ensure they're not overcooking.
7. Once the timer beeps, allow the bombs to cool before taking them out of the basket or tray as they might be a little too soft to move when they're too hot.
8. Serve on a platter with toothpicks!

Salmon Canape Tarts

Nothing says "classy dinner party" (or "retro dinner party") like salmon and cream cheese tarts. These are for people in a rush or those who can't bear fiddling with homemade pastry - they use store bought tart cases! No shame in that.

Serves: makes 20
Time: approximately 20 minutes

Ingredients:
- 20 store bought mini tart cases (the really small ones)
- 5 eggs, lightly beaten
- 1/3 cup heavy cream
- Salt and pepper
- 3 oz. smoked salmon, lox or gravlax (depending on what you have and what you call it!)
- 7 oz. plain cream cheese, broken or cut into 20 small pieces
- Fresh dill

Method:
1. Place the tart cases into your air fryer basket or tray. It's easier to fill them when they're already in their cooking vessel as they can be very hard to transfer without spilling.
2. Beat together the eggs, cream, salt and pepper in a pourable measuring jug.
3. Pour the egg mixture into the tarts, about ⅔ the way up the side of the tart case.
4. Place a piece of salmon and a piece of cream cheese into each tart, nestled into the egg.
5. Place the basket or tray into the air fryer.
6. Set the temperature to 360 degrees Fahrenheit and the time to 8 minutes.
7. Check on the tarts at the 5-minute mark to ensure they're not overcooking.
8. Once the timer beeps, carefully take the tarts out of the air fryer and leave them to cool before serving on a platter with a sprinkle of fresh dill as a garnish.

Desserts

The sweetest section for last! The air fryer isn't only great for savory dishes but it's fantastic for sweet treats too. Here you will find chocolate, caramel, fruit and baked goods.

Chocolate and Strawberry Cake

A classic chocolate cake with some special additions. If you don't have freeze-dried strawberries just use frozen ones. Use any kind of chocolate chips you prefer or a mixture of all three!

Serves: makes 1 cake
Time: approximately 40 minutes

Ingredients:
- 1 ½ cups plain flour
- 1/3 cup cocoa powder
- 2 tsp. baking powder
- ¾ cup white sugar
- ¼ cup brown sugar
- 2/3 cup butter
- 2 tsp. vanilla extract
- 1 cup milk
- 1 tsp baking soda
- 2 eggs
- 1 cup freeze-dried strawberries
- 1 cup chocolate chips (dark, milk or white)

To serve with:
- 1 batch of chocolate ganache or chocolate buttercream
- Fresh strawberries to garnish

Method:
1. Prepare a cake tin by lining with baking powder, or you can simply use your air fryer basket if it's appropriate.
2. Sift the flour, cocoa and baking powder into a large bowl.
3. Place both sugars, butter, vanilla, milk and baking soda into a microwave-safe bowl and microwave at increments of 30 seconds until the butter has melted and the ingredients are incorporated, leave to cool a little.
4. Add the eggs to the butter mixture and whisk to combine.
5. Pour the wet ingredients into the dry ingredients and fold to combine.
6. Fold the strawberries and chocolate chips into the batter.
7. Pour the batter into your prepared tin or basket and pop it into the air fryer.
8. Set the temperature at 340 degrees Fahrenheit and set the time at 30 minutes.
9. Once the timer beeps, check to ensure the cake is cooked and springs back when touched.
10. Ice with ganache or buttercream frosting, and top with fresh strawberries.

Cheaters Cookie Bars with Added Chocolate

This is the ultimate lazy dessert. Instead of making cookie dough we are embracing the store bought stuff! But to make it extra naughty we are adding even more chocolate. Just go with it.

Oh, and these are GREAT to make with kids as a birthday treat or sleepover snack.

Serves: makes approximately 12 bars
Time: approximately 30 minutes

Ingredients:
- 1 package store bought cookie dough
- 1 small packet of M&M's
- 1 small packet of Maltesers
- 1 small packet of Milk Duds

Method:
1. Line a tray with baking paper - ensure it fits into your air fryer. Or simply use your air fryer basket if appropriate.
2. Press half of the cookie dough into your lined tray or basket.
3. Scatter the M&M's, Maltesers and Milk Duds over the dough.
4. Press the remaining dough onto the chocolate treats and place the tray/basket into the air fryer.
5. Set the temperature to 360 degrees Fahrenheit and set the time to 20 minutes.
6. At the 10-minute mark, check the bars to ensure they're not overcooking. If you like them super soft and fudgy, cook them for a little less.
7. Serve warm with a glass of milk!

Sticky Cinnamon Rolls

These rolls are more like fancy scones than real cinnamon rolls. But I like to turn to this recipe when I don't feel like working with yeast and waiting around for the rising process. Slather some vanilla glaze on top with a side of ice cream and no one will be complaining.

Serves: makes 12 rolls
Time: approximately 35 minutes

Ingredients:
- 2 cups flour
- 3 Tbsp. white sugar
- 2 ½ tsp. baking powder
- 1 tsp. ground cinnamon
- Pinch of salt
- 2/3 cup cold butter, cubed
- ¾ cup heavy cream
- 1 egg
- 2 tsp. vanilla extract

Filling:
- 1/3 cup butter, softened
- ¾ cup brown sugar mixed with 3 tsp. ground cinnamon

Optional glaze (you can also use cream cheese frosting):
- 2 cups icing (confectioners') sugar
- 1 Tbsp. vanilla extract
- Enough heavy cream to create a smooth, spreadable consistency

Method:
1. Combine the flour, sugar, baking powder, salt and cinnamon in a large bowl
2. Add the butter to the bowl and rub it in with your hands until it appears sandy and crumbly.
3. Whisk together the cream, egg and vanilla extract.
4. Add the cream mixture to the dry ingredients and stir to combine.
5. Flour a clean board or bench and tip the dough out onto the surface.
6. Knead the dough a few times until smooth, then roll it into a rectangle (about ½ inch).
7. Spread the softened butter over the dough, then sprinkle the brown sugar and cinnamon over the butter.

8. Roll the dough into a log lengthwise (i.e. hold the long side of the rectangle and roll from there).
9. Slice the dough into 12 rolls and place into your air fryer basket or tray (line with paper or spray with oil spray if you're concerned about sticking).
10. Set the temperature to 360 degrees Fahrenheit and set the time to 20 minutes.
11. Once the timer beeps, check the rolls, they may not be done but it pays to undercook then put them back in rather than overcook in the first place. Pop them back in until they're just cooked.
12. Remove the cooked rolls from the air fryer, leave to cool slightly, then pour the glaze or frosting over the top.
13. Serve warm!

Citrus Cheesecake

A plain cheesecake with the addition of sunny, fresh-tasting lemon zest. This cheesecake needs to be made overnight or in the morning as it needs at least 6 hours in the fridge to cool and fully set.

Serves: makes 1 cheesecake
Time: approximately 1 hour and 15 minutes to prepare and cook, then overnight to cool

Ingredients:
- 9 oz. graham crackers, crushed
- 4 oz. butter, melted
- 18 oz. plain cream cheese
- 3 eggs
- 4 Tbsp. white sugar
- 1 Tbsp. vanilla extract
- Zest of 2 lemons

Method:
1. Prepare a cake tin by lining with baking paper, ensure it fits into your air fryer. Or you can use the basket in your air fryer if appropriate.
2. Stir together the graham crackers and melted butter and press into the lined tin or basket.
3. Place the cream cheese, eggs, sugar, vanilla and lemon zest into a large bowl and beat with egg beaters until smooth and combined.
4. Pour the cream cheese mixture into the basket or tin, on top of the graham cracker base.
5. Place the cheesecake into the air fryer and set the temperature to 340 degrees Fahrenheit and set the time to 40 minutes.
6. Once the timer beeps, check to ensure the cheesecake is just set but still a bit wobbly.
7. Allow the cheesecake to cool on the bench then place it into the fridge to cool overnight.
8. Serve plain or with lemon curd!

Stone Fruit Pie

You can use any stone fruits in season for this pie. Plums, nectarines and peaches can all be combined for a beautiful, sweet, warming dessert encased in pastry and hopefully with a big scoop of ice cream.

Serves: makes 1 pie
Time: approximately 1 hour

Ingredients:
- Homemade or store bought sweet shortcrust pastry or pie casing, enough for one pie. You can even use a ready-formed pie case too
- 1 ½ lbs. stone fruit, stones removed, flesh cut into even wedges or chunks
- 1 Tbsp. vanilla extract
- 1/3 cup water
- 2 Tbsp. white sugar
- 2 Tbsp. butter
- 2 tsp. cornstarch mixed with 1 Tbsp. water

Method:
1. Prepare your pie pan or air fryer basket by greasing with butter or oil spray. Line the tin with pastry. Pop the pie case into the air fryer and cook for 5 minutes at 390 degrees Fahrenheit to precook the raw pastry. If using a store bought, ready-formed, pre-cooked pie case then you don't have to do anything!
2. Place the fruits, vanilla, water, sugar, butter and cornstarch mixture into a large saucepan over a medium heat and whisk as the butter melts and the fruit begins to soften.
3. Tip the fruit mixture into the pie casing and pop it back into the air fryer.
4. Set the temperature to 390 degrees Fahrenheit and set the time to 30 minutes.
5. Once the timer beeps, check to ensure the fruit is soft and the edge of the pastry is golden.
6. Serve with ice cream and/or heavy cream!

Baked Apples

This is a reasonably healthy dessert. I mean, it does have butter and sugar... but it also has an apple! To totally negate the healthiness I like to serve it with butterscotch sauce and vanilla ice cream.

Serves: 2
Time: approximately 40 minutes

Ingredients:
- 2 Granny Smith apples, core removed but not right to the bottom, leave the very bottom intact so the filling doesn't fall out
- 2 Tbsp. butter, cold
- 4 Tbsp. brown sugar
- 4 Tbsp. crushed walnuts
- 2 Tbsp. sultanas
- 1 tsp. cinnamon

Method:
1. Place the butter, brown sugar, walnuts, sultanas and cinnamon into a small bowl and rub the mixture together with your fingers until it resembles a crumble or streusel.
2. Place the apples into your air fryer basket or tray.
3. Stuff the apples (into the hole you made when you took the core out) with the filling mixture. If there's any leftover you can reserve it and sprinkle it over the top after the apples have been cooked.
4. Place the tray or basket into the air fryer, set the temperature to 390 degrees Fahrenheit and set the time to 30 minutes.
5. Once the timer beeps, check to ensure the apples are nice and soft and pop them back in for a few more minutes if they need a bit more time.
6. Serve with butterscotch sauce, ice cream or cream!

S'mores

Time for s'mores! Another kid-friendly recipe. Be prepared for a major sugar hit as they're packed with all things sticky and sweet.

Serves: makes 8 s'mores
Time: approximately 10 minutes

Ingredients:
- 8 graham cracker sheets, snapped in half
- 16 large marshmallows
- 16 squares each of dark, milk and white chocolate
- Optional: raspberry jam (I like the fruity tang)
- Baking paper

Method:
1. Lay the graham cracker halves onto a board.
2. If using the jam, spread it onto eight of the graham cracker halves.
3. Place two marshmallows onto eight of the graham cracker halves.
4. Place the chocolate (two squares of each) onto the cracker with the marshmallows.
5. Place the remaining graham crackers on top to create eight sandwiches.
6. Wrap each s'more in baking paper like a little parcel.
7. Place the s'more parcels into your air fryer basket or tray.
8. Set the temperature to 300 degrees Fahrenheit and set the time to 6 minutes.
9. Once the timer beeps, check the s'mores to ensure they are nice and melted!
10. Serve with a cup of hot chocolate.

Brownies

These brownies have walnuts and chunks of white chocolate hiding amongst the gooey, chocolate goodness. They are the REAL brownies which have chocolate melted into the batter.

Serves: makes 12 brownies
Time: approximately 30 minutes

Ingredients:
- 7 oz. dark chocolate
- 7 oz. butter
- ¾ cup white sugar
- 3 eggs
- 2 tsp. vanilla extract
- ¾ cup flour
- ¼ cup cocoa powder
- 1 cup chopped walnuts
- 1 cup white chocolate chips

Method:
1. Line a brownie pan or the basket of your air fryer with baking paper.
2. Place the chocolate, butter and sugar into a saucepan and place over a low heat and keep stirring as it melts together and forms a smooth mixture.
3. Take the chocolate mixture off the heat and leave to cool slightly.
4. Add the eggs and vanilla extract to the mixture and whisk to combine.
5. Sift the flour and cocoa powder into the mixture and stir to combine.
6. Fold the walnuts and white chocolate into the batter.
7. Pour the batter into your prepared pan or basket and place into the air fryer.
8. Set the temperature to 370 degrees Fahrenheit and set the time to 15 minutes.
9. Once the timer beeps, check the brownies. They might be a little underdone for your liking so pop them back in for a few more minutes.
10. Serve with ice cream!

Berry and White Chocolate Mini Cheesecakes

These cheesecakes are small, cute and very addictive. They have a ginger base and the filling is dotted with juicy berries and sweet white chocolate. You will need 4 4-inch pie or tart pans.

Serves: makes 4 mini cheesecakes
Time: approximately 4 hours (which includes 3 hours of cooling and refrigeration)

Ingredients:
- 4.5 oz. graham crackers, crushed
- 1 tsp. ground ginger
- 1 Tbsp. chopped crystallized ginger
- 2 oz. butter, melted
- 9 oz. plain cream cheese
- 2 eggs
- 2 Tbsp. white sugar
- 1 cup mixed frozen berries
- ¾ cup white chocolate chips

Method:
1. Prepare your tins by greasing them thoroughly with softened butter.
2. Place the graham cracker crumbs, ground ginger, crystallized ginger and butter into a bowl and stir to combine.
3. Press the graham cracker mixture into the prepared tins.
4. Place the cream cheese, eggs and sugar into a bowl and beat with egg beaters until smooth, thick and combined.
5. Fold the berries and white chocolate into the cream cheese mixture.
6. Spoon the cream cheese mixture into the tins, on top of the graham cracker base.
7. Place the cheesecakes into the air fryer, set the temperature to 350 degrees Fahrenheit and set the time to 15 minutes.
8. Once the timer beeps, check to ensure the cheesecakes are just set but still a little wobbly.
9. Leave them to cool on the bench before popping them into the fridge for a few hours before serving.
10. Serve with whipped cream and a few extra fresh berries scattered on top.

Cheats Apple and Caramel Crumble Cake

Here's another recipe with store bought ingredients. This time, we are using a boxed cake mix and bought caramel! But don't feel bad, we are adding apples and crumble... so technically we are making it from scratch... sort of.

Serves: makes 1 cake
Time: approximately 40 minutes

Ingredients:
- 1 vanilla box cake
- 2 apples, peeled and cut into slices
- 3 oz. butter, melted
- ½ cup brown sugar
- 1 tsp. cinnamon
- ½ cup flour
- 1 cup store bought toffee or caramel sauce

Method:
1. Prepare a cake tin or your air fryer basket by lining with baking paper.
2. Prepare the crumble by mixing the butter, sugar, cinnamon and flour until it forms a crumble/streusel texture.
3. Prepare the boxed cake mix batter according to the instructions (don't bake it yet!).
4. Pour the batter into your prepared cake tin or basket.
5. Lay the apple slices onto the batter.
6. Pour the caramel sauce over the apples.
7. Sprinkle the crumble over the sauce.
8. Place the cake into the air fryer, set the temperature to 390 degrees Fahrenheit and set the time to 30 minutes.
9. At the 20-minute mark, check the cake to ensure it's not overcooking or drying out. Use your discretion to decide when the cake is ready.
10. Serve with extra caramel sauce and vanilla ice cream!

Chocolate and Banana Brioche Sandwiches

If you've made any of the breakfast recipes which include brioche, you may have some left over. Good news! You can use it to make these amazing, gooey dessert sandwiches. Chocolate and bananas melt together between two buttery pieces of brioche. Again... serve with ice cream!

Serves: makes 2 brioche sandwiches (great for couples and date nights)
Time: approximately 30 minutes

Ingredients:
- 4 slices of brioche
- 1 Tbsp. melted butter
- 6 oz. dark, milk or white chocolate, or a mixture of all, broken into chunks
- 1 banana, sliced

Method:
1. Brush the brioche slices with melted butter.
2. Layer two of the brioche slices with chocolate chunks and banana slices.
3. Place the remaining two brioche slices onto the banana and chocolate to create two sandwiches.
4. Place the sandwiches into the air fryer basket or tray.
5. Set the temperature to 380 degrees Fahrenheit and set the time to 15 minutes.
6. At the 7-minute mark, turn the sandwiches over.
7. Once the timer beeps, carefully remove the sandwiches from the air fryer, slice in half and serve on a plate with vanilla ice cream!

Conclusion

I hope that your air fryer is giving you lots of joy, time and most importantly, tasty dishes. Please feel free to adjust and alter these recipes, or simply use them as a springboard of inspiration for your own creations!

Putting together interesting and unexpected ingredients is so much fun and can be really rewarding, so get creative in your kitchen.

Always remember to clean your air fryer and accessories according to the instructions and safety precautions after each cooking adventure.

Happy cooking!

Made in the USA
Middletown, DE
02 November 2018